Peace in an Unlikely Place

A Story of Triumph over Adversity

Crystal Owonubi

ISBN: 978-1496083791

To Whitney, Micah, and Jayden

In the past we also were foolish. We did not obey, we were wrong, and we were slaves to many things our bodies wanted and enjoyed. We spent our lives doing evil and being jealous. People hated us, and we hated each other. But when the kindness and love of God our Savior was shown, he saved us because of his mercy. It was not because of good deeds we did to be right with him. He saved us through the washing that made us new people through the Holy Spirit. God poured out richly upon us that Holy Spirit through Jesus Christ our Savior. Being made right with God by his grace, we could have the hope of receiving the life that never ends. Titus 3:3-8

I know how to live when I am poor, and I know how to live when I have plenty. I have learned the secret of being happy at any time in everything that happens, when I have enough to eat and when I go hungry, when I have more than I need and when I do not have enough. I can do all things through Christ, because he gives me strength. Philippians 4:12-13

As you read about my journey of living in Nigeria and how God changed my life, I pray that you will be inspired and will be able to see the works of our Father, Jesus Christ!

Many people have told me that I should write a story about my journey to Nigeria, how I ended up in such a faraway place after growing up in a small town in southern Arkansas. I spent years talking about writing a book about my life; but I needed an ending, a story of success, or a testimony. Now God has given me that portion of my story. I could not rest until I put into writing the details of how God changed my life and took me through heartaches, happiness, rejection, struggles, pain, hardships, love, peace, and—most of all—endurance.

Many others also told me how I have inspired their lives and that I have become a strong woman. This has given me great joy during the many times that I struggled with not being able to go back to my home country that I adored so much, because I wanted to keep my family together. I never knew I had this amount of strength and endurance. It is said, "Whatever doesn't hurt you makes you stronger." That means physically as well as emotionally.

A Nigerian woman I didn't know wanted to meet me. She heard about me through someone who also had never met me. My husband Albert told me that my reputation precedes me. When I went to the house to meet this woman, she gave me a huge hug, then looked at me and said, "You have such a high tolerance to be able to stay in Nigeria for this long, and you should be in the Guinness World Book of Records." That gave me a whole new sense of strength because she recognized that what I did was not easy for one day. That was like telling a soldier "Thank you for serving and fighting for our country." All along I was fighting for something: I refused to let the devil break my family apart regardless of our circumstances. I felt like I fought a battle with the devil who wanted to destroy me and my family.

Tributes

"I will write a book of my story!" This must have been the umpteenth time I had heard Crystal say this. "Sure honey," I replied, "You really have a lot to tell." This was the reflexive response I had become conditioned to giving my wife.

This book by my wife, Crystal Owonubi, is a tale of joys and sorrows, and the ability of God to heal any situation. I would know this—I think I am a key character in her book.

Crystal has gone through a continual series of highs and lows in her life. I must admit that, after being married to her for several years, I see clearly that she has a deep passion for her life to affect the lives of others for good. People who find themselves in situations that are seemingly hopeless will find this book a story that can give them the hope of a second chance.

This book may not be an accurate depiction of every single incident that has occurred in Crystal's life; however, it captures the essence of her entire story. Something of a grass-to-grace account, the hand of God can be clearly seen when we go through the pages of these memoirs of my wife.

Crystal has become a kind and loving woman, with enough inner strength to pull a nation together. She has gone from absolute disdain of this life to loving every moment that God, by his grace, has given us to live upon this earth. Her attitude towards situations is not only something she writes about, but also what she lives day by day. I remember the day I said to Crystal; "Would you follow me if I had to return to Nigeria?" Her reply was, "I would follow you wherever you go." Those few words have been lived out for the past several years by my sweetheart.

When we first met, we were young and very stupid; we had a very myopic outlook on life and had very little direction. We really were irrational and irresponsible. The funny thing is that we were wise in our own eyes, and thought we had everything under control. Years later, I see the folly in our past and realize that it was all part of the journey. I also now realize how little we have under our own control. We see the hand of a great God, who is willing and able to gently and steadily move us closer towards his destiny and purpose for our lives on earth.

Crystal's life is a life of purpose. The simplicity and innocence of her writing, along with clarity in communication, commands such powerful emotion for the reader. This beautiful young lady, with whom I fell in love several years back, has blossomed into the girl of my dreams. I'm extremely proud of the effort and commitment she has made to deliver this wonderful work, and I'm certain that this book has the ability to make you laugh, make you cry, make you think about the things that really matter, and hopefully and most importantly, help you have a better understanding of how God operates in our lives. He did touch Crystal, and spurred a great change.

Finally, I must admit that the process of writing a book such as this is very involved. Crystal put her heart into it, and I'm certain it will be a favorite of many. I thank you so much, Crystal, for helping even me to believe in myself again, and realizing that I have a God of second chances. I also thank you for standing by me through the greatest challenges of my life.

This is not the end of the story; in fact, this is only the beginning. I look forward to spending the rest of my life here on earth with my lovely wife Crystal. I am sure that her writing will continue to inspire millions of people across the globe, and that our God will be glorified!

—Albert Owonubi

When I first met Crystal, she had been in Nigeria for just a few weeks. She sensed a kindred spirit in me, and asked the most important question first: "What on earth do you eat here?" Crystal had no desire to be in Nigeria, but God had other plans for her. In Nigeria her faith matured; her marriage stabilized, and her children knew a loving, stable home. Although finances were tight and she missed the comforts of America, Crystal was able to break free from generational dysfunction and truly find peace in Nigeria. - —
—Mary Beth Oyebade

As an American woman also married to a Nigerian I was excited to read Crystal's story, and it didn't disappoint. This is a truly entertaining story of one woman's unusual and exciting life, but it's even more than that. This is a story of God's grace and redemption. God has done an amazing work in Crystal's life, and her testimony of His work will inspire anyone who hears it. When I finished reading Crystal's story I thought of the first couple verses of Isaiah 61—especially verse 3:

"…and provide for those who grieve in Zion—to bestow on them

a crown of beauty instead of ashes, the oil of joy instead of mourning, and a garment of praise instead of a spirit of despair. They will be called oaks of righteousness, a planting of the Lord for the display of his splendor."
Crystal is displaying the splendor of God's grace in her story, and I think it's wonderful!!!
—Sarah Ajero

Crystal's story is an example of choosing well. Her childhood went from happy to tragic. Her teen years were filled with poor choices that led her down many unhappy paths. Her early adult life continued to be unsettled. Finally she was faced with the choice of giving up on her marriage, or going to live in the developing country of Nigeria with her husband. That life offered nothing but hardships in her American mind.
It is thrilling to see how Crystal came to realize that mere comforts pale in comparison to the caring relationships she came to love in Nigeria. God has done a good work in her life, and the legacy she has chosen for her children will be seen for generations. She has overcome a life of self-centeredness and has found that caring for others first brings great satisfaction. Forgiving those who have hurt her and moving on in God's grace rounds out the picture of Crystal's transformed life.
This is a compelling story of triumph over adversity.
—Sandi Wallestad

Quite an epistle, an insightful blend of family, race, socio-cultural and religious exposé. So sincere.
—Ayodeji Owonubi

"This book is a picture of a life transformed by the power of Christ's love. It is my joy and pleasure to be a close friend of Albert and Crystal Owonubi. Read *"Peace in an Unlikely Place"* and be amazed by His grace!"
—LaVonna Ennis, missionary

The book "Peace in an Unlikely Place" is the story of a young lady who from childhood had encounters that tended to impair her destiny until she had an encounter with the unchangeable changer, our Lord Jesus Christ, who took her from her zero position in life to a hero position. And to think that this happened in an unlikely place, Nigeria, Africa; a continent branded as a land of disease, despair, and death shows that God can do great things anywhere and anytime.

—Reverend Godswill Israel

You know as missionaries we choose to live in difficult places where most westerners would not want to go. We have a choice, but what if you and your family had to leave your comfort zone (your country) and didn't have choice. The book "Peace in an Unlikely Place" is the story of one woman (a friend) who had to make a choice, her family or her country! She lost the only way of life she knew but found a new culture and found a strong woman she never knew existed, her self!

—Rick Jara, missionary

Author's Notes

Some of the names in this book have been changed in order to maintain the dignity and privacy of those individuals.

This book may not tell every single detail of my experiences, but it captures the essence of my story. Everything I have written about Nigeria is from my own point of view from living in Jos for many years. It is my hope and prayer that things will not be taken the wrong way and will not offend or hurt anyone. This is a true story and nothing is made up.

FOREWORD

When my wife and I first met Crystal, she had one goal in life: to get Albert's visa and return to the United States. She was shy, frightened and experiencing culture shock. We were thrilled to watch the transformation of this young couple. Albert is an industrious young man dedicated to God and to his family. Crystal's goals are now to be pleasing to God, to be a true helpmate to Albert, to train Whitney and Micah to be responsible adults with a secure relationship with God, and to reach out to those in need who surround her.

Crystal did not share her past easily and freely when we first met. Her story came to us in bits and pieces. When put together, hers is an incredible tale taking you through the stages of pain, anger, despair and desperation, which ultimately led her to peace through Jesus Christ. No longer is she frustrated and tense; she is now fulfilled and triumphant. Her journey has brought her to the discovery that her self-worth is not found in her family roots, but in the fact that she is the daughter of the King of Kings!

Scott Ennis, President
Evangel Theological Seminary
Jos, Nigeria

1

That day in the summer of 2005 was like any other day for my husband Albert, our 4-year-old daughter Whitney, and me. We were on our way to drop Whitney at preschool before we began our busy day of work. Normally, Albert would drop Whitney at school in the morning while I would go to school at Chattahoochee Technical College from 8:00 to 10:00 before going to work at 11:00. That day I didn't have class, so we decided to ride together to drop her at school. Instead of catching a few extra hours of sleep, I chose to go along just to get a few minutes together as a family in the car. It happened to be the end of the school year, so we stopped by the grocery store to purchase some flowers for Whitney's teacher to show appreciation.

As we stopped at a traffic light, behind us was a police car that pulled us over. Unknown to us, our brake light was out. We didn't think much of being pulled over since we hadn't done anything wrong.

The police officer stepped out of his car, walked up to the driver side and said to Albert, "Sir, can I see your driver's license and registration please."

The officer collected the requested documents, and walked back to his vehicle to do a search to make sure Albert had no warrants, which is a normal process for an American police officer. Luckily, he had no warrants, although he did have one thing that could send him away. We never knew that the police and Immigration Department worked together.

As the officer walked back to our vehicle, he said, "Sir, I need you to step out of the car."

As Albert opened the car door, slowly attempting to get out of the car while wondering what was happening, the police officer pulled him by the arm dragging him out of the car as if Albert were resisting. I could tell that the officer was not fond of seeing a white woman and a black man together. He appeared to be nervous, perhaps wondering how Albert was going to react. The officer's nervousness was shown by the way he pulled Albert out of the car instead of giving him a chance to come out on his own.

As they both stepped to the back of the car, I turned my head to see if I could figure out why Albert was asked to get out of the car. I happened to hear one word from the officer's mouth: *"deported."*

My heart stopped. As I opened my car door and started to get out of the car to see what was happening, the police officer looked at me and said, "Madam, step back inside the vehicle."

I am not sure what I wanted to do at that moment. I knew the police officer had no idea of the heartache he was about to cause; he was just doing his job. I was reeling in shock as I became aware of what was about to happen to my husband.

Albert and I both knew that his school visa had expired and he had overstayed without authorization which is reason for deportation. We both had fears of it happening one day. We had thought of beginning the process of filing for his citizenship since we were married, but we had fears of deportation and being separated as a family since he had already overstayed. We were sure that as soon as we started the filing process, they would look for him and deport him immediately. It was just a horrible situation to be in, like either choice would be wrong.

Albert had asked me at an earlier time that if he had to return to Nigeria, would I follow him. I replied, "Yes, of course!" without putting much thought into it. I just knew that I never wanted to be separated from my husband. There was something about him that I fell in love with when I first met him and from that moment on I never wanted to be away from him.

The police officer put Albert in the back seat of his car like a criminal. Since he had overstayed his visa, he had committed a crime according to the United States Immigration Laws; but in my eyes I knew that he was not a criminal and did not deserve to be in the back seat or to be taken away from his family. Albert has always been a gentle, caring, and loving man. Some may read this and say he was an illegal immigrant and they should deport him. I know the laws of immigration and would never condone breaking the law. However, this was my husband, the father of my child, and my best friend being taken away from me, far away to a foreign country that I knew absolutely nothing about. Albert and I never spoke much about his country other than when he told me about what happened with the government in Nigeria during the time that his mother sent him to America to go to school.

We were allowed a few seconds to speak while he sat in the back seat of the police car, but with so little time there was not much to discuss, other than to say our goodbyes as tears rolled down our faces.

Albert said, "I love you!"

"I love you, too," I said, "but what is going to happen to us?" I felt like I was going to hyperventilate or faint.

I had always known that if he were deported, Albert would be barred from the United States for ten years. I thought to myself, *Just like that, my husband is here one day and now he's gone!* I couldn't imagine waiting ten years for him to come back home. Would I leave my country and follow him to Nigeria or would I stay in my country and wait for him?

2

When I was just a small girl, my mother would wake me up for school in the mornings by pulling my toes and making them pop. I would shout, "Stop it, Mom!" while laughing and enjoying my mother's laugh. She was a woman full of jokes and laughter and was loved for her peculiar personality.

"Ahhhhhh!" I screamed in fear. Someone was in the window of the living room holding a flashlight and wearing a mask on their head while my brother Billy and I were watching television. Then we heard the sound of our mother laughing hysterically when she saw that we were cowering in fear of the boogie man.

One day when Billy had his friends over, they were sitting at the table eating cake. Mom leaned over to clean the table off and one of her breasts was hanging out. She casually asked his friends, "Do you want another piece of cake?" while trying not to burst into laughter again. As soon as Billy's friend looked over and noticed, his mouth dropped wide open and his eyes bulged out.

I shouted, "Mom, what are you doing?" I couldn't believe what she had just done. I was so humiliated.

Although she did crazy things, she was a beautiful woman with her long black hair, small figure, and big smile. She decorated my room fit for a princess and bought me many dolls and stuffed animals. I could spend hours in my room alone pretending to teach my baby dolls, imitating my teacher or the librarian from school, labeling each book in my room pretending that my dolls were checking out books in the make-believe library.

Mom entered me in beauty pageants when I was just a small girl, dressing me up in beautiful dresses. I won several trophies during the many pageants in which I participated.

She took my older brother to play softball where he also won several trophies. Mom kept all of our trophies in our rooms. She even sewed the clothes that we wore to school. Many of my friends would come over to our house to play with me. The doghouse in our front yard was so big that it became a perfect place for us to climb up on; where we could sit on top to imagine we were in charge of the world. My friend and I would bring along books, toys, a blanket, and food to have a picnic. I was a happy little girl.

Mom took us to the Assemblies of God Church just two minutes down the road from our house. She always sang in church with her friend. Since Mom sang in church, I decided that I wanted to sing too. I wanted to be just like my mommy. So my friend April and I would sing together in church: "At the cross, at the cross, where I first saw the light, and the burden of my heart rolled away!"

On the last Sunday of each month, a potluck dinner was held at the church; and every member would prepare one of their tastiest dishes. Mom also brought her coffee cups, and they had a teddy bear or a fish attached inside the bottom of the cup. She brought the pastor some coffee in one of the cups, and then waited off to the side to see what his reaction would be when he got to the bottom of his cup. As the pastor stared into the cup, Mom doubled over with laughter to see his reaction. The pastor laughed saying, "Oh, Rita!"

Even when Mom didn't go to church, I would always make sure that the pastor's wife picked me up on Sunday. I would call her on the phone and ask, "Can you pick me up for church on Sunday?"

She would reply, "Yes, Crystal, we will be there to pick you up at 8:00 sharp!"

The pastor and his wife would pull up in the driveway and honk, and I would come running out. My father never did go to church with us except on Christmas Day. I never heard him say one word about Jesus Christ.

My mother was a stay-at-home-mom, taking care of the house and us kids. The kids in the neighborhood always loved to come to our house because our mother was loads of fun. In addition, our dad made sure we had plenty of entertainment: a dune buggy, our own motorcycles, bicycles, a computer, and pit bulls as pets. The pit bulls would fight and people from the neighborhood would come to watch them.

We also loved going to our friends' houses to play, but if we started going to their homes too much, Mom would say, "You're going to wear out your welcome if you don't stop going there every day!" She wanted us to spend more time at our house, and she didn't want the neighbors to get tired of us.

Once while riding my little yellow motorcycle (which was exactly the right size for me) through the neighbor's backyard, I crashed. I didn't even tell my parents. I went to lie down on the living room floor to rest from the impact. Billy came to me and said, "Are you okay? You don't look well."

I replied slowly, "My stomach hurts. I drove my motorcycle through the neighbor's backyard and hit a pothole and the handlebar poked into my stomach!"

Billy said, "Sorry, but you'll be okay!" And I was okay after a short rest.

As a family, we would often ride our motorcycles together through the woods. Since I was the youngest, my motorcycle was the smallest. I always dragged my feet on the ground while driving to keep my balance because I was afraid of tipping over. It reminded me of the story of the three little bears, except there were four of us. I was always slower than the rest of the family, and one day they hid from me in the woods nearby just to see my reaction when I realized I was all alone.

I stopped and looked around saying to myself, "I guess they forgot about me and now I don't know how I will find my way back home!" All along they were watching me talk to myself. They came out of the woods laughing and Mom said, "Oh Sissy, we wouldn't leave you alone!"

My dad had lots of interests. He loved to fish so he always had the latest bass boat. He had a pool table in the den, so when his friends came over he could shoot pool with them. Dad bought a camper and we often spent weekends at the lake swimming while he went fishing. We loved the delicious catfish that he fried for us. One time we even had a pet raccoon, but it attacked my dad so he killed it.

Every year we would go to Sarcoxie, Missouri, to visit our Grandma and Grandpa, dad's parents. Dad said, "Kids, pack your things, we are going to see Grandma!" We would wake up in the wee hours of the morning to get an early start in Daddy's Oldsmobile truck.

Daddy always said that an Oldsmobile was a much better brand than Ford, because Ford stands for "Found on Road Dead." I suppose his conclusion came from working on so many different vehicles all those years.

Dad would drive and Mom would sit right next to him in the truck, while Billy and I sat on the other side. Billy and I would become bored and tired of being inside the truck, cramped up next to each other for so long. "Mom, are we almost there?" we asked over and over again.

"No, we are not almost there. Would you just ride and keep quiet?" she replied in frustration.

My grandparents lived on a farm with horses and cattle. They would slaughter a cow for us every year, and it was enough beef to last the entire year. My Grandma always had a kitchen full of the best home-cooked foods for us to eat: mashed potatoes, homemade bread and jam, corn, fried chicken and turkey. She would bake several different pies, but my favorite was chocolate. "Crystal, I made the chocolate pie especially for you!" Grandma said.

Oh, how I loved Grandma and Grandpa Murphree. Grandma always let me help her in the kitchen when she made homemade biscuits.

Grandpa would sit in his recliner listening to people talk on the CB or amateur radio while frequently answering and saying, "10-4, 10-4".

Grandpa had a lot of hound dogs and often took them hunting. One day I went to see the dogs and accidentally let them out of their cage. I could tell Grandpa was upset with me when he shouted in his otherwise gentle southern accent, "Crystal, are you the one that let those dogs out of the cage?" It took some time, but he gathered up the dogs again.

One time Grandma took us to the zoo to see the dinosaurs. Yes, the dinosaurs! To this day, I don't understand how it was going to be possible. As it turned out, we didn't even go inside the zoo because I got grease on the back of my pants from sitting in the back seat of Grandma's friend's car. I was too humiliated to go inside the zoo like that, afraid that someone would think that I pooped on myself. Grandma kept saying, "Crystal, these people are never going to see you again!"

I pleaded, "Please, don't make me go in there like this!" I refused to go inside and was willing to sit in the car while they went in, but she wasn't going to leave me alone. So we all went back home again.

Dad's only sister worked at "Justin Boots" in Joplin, Missouri, and every time we visited they would buy each of us a new pair of boots. When it was time to go back home, we would go back with all kinds of gifts from the family: the meat, new boots, toys, and baked goods made by Grandma. It was a happy time.

Dad served in the United States Navy, but Mom had quit school in the eighth grade. Dad worked hard to provide for us, while Mom worked hard to take care of the house and us kids. Dad had a job at General Motors for many years, and then he worked for UPS as a mechanic and eventually retired from there.

Dad grew up in West Helena, Arkansas, while Mom grew up in Farmington, and my brother and I grew up in Bauxite. Bauxite was a small town with a population of about 4,000 people. Mom would have to drive about twenty minutes to get to the next town just to buy groceries or take care of any business. Going to town with Mom in the station wagon was always fun because we got to sit in the back seat that faced backwards.

There were no black people in Bauxite, only whites. Pine Haven Elementary School consisted of all white students except for one girl named Kaylee that had a black father and a white mother.

School wasn't too far from our house, and the bus would pick us up and drop us off every day. One day after school I got off the bus, and when I got to the house I saw my brother riding his bike. I asked Mom, "How come you didn't pick me up from school, too?"

She was so tickled and laughed at me saying, "He rode the bus home with you. Didn't you see him on the bus?"

Both Billy and I were puzzled that I rode the bus all the way home and never saw him or heard him and didn't even see him get off the bus. I don't know where my mind was that I managed to miss all of that. We enjoyed riding the bus to school because it gave us extra time with friends.

The bus driver was always so sweet to us kids. She saw me crying one day and asked, "What's wrong Crystal?"

"I have a loose tooth." I was tired of that tooth dangling in my mouth and irritating me, so I needed someone to help me get it out. I said, "Billy, please help me get my tooth out." Right then and there he punched me in the mouth and knocked out my tooth! Even though I cried, I was still relieved that it was over. The bus driver was about to punish Billy after seeing in her rearview mirror what he had done to me. "No! Mrs. Robinson," I said, "it's okay because I told him to do it!" She wasn't sure if it was true or if I was just trying to cover for him.

Billy often tried to aggravate me to a point that I would cry until my head was pounding. He would even flick boogers in my hair. One day I was so fed up with him that I took a huge rock and threw it right at his head. "You better leave me alone!" I shouted. I was terrified that I was going to get a whipping by Mom with her big stick for throwing the rock at Billy. I ran and hid behind the couch and soothed myself by eating sugar cubes, which were a favorite of mine.

Billy was screaming, "I'm going to kill you!"

Billy would throw rocks at me while we waited for the bus to pick us up for school; he said he wanted to see me dance like Michael Jackson. While some kids had bullies in school, I had a bully living in the house with me. I frequently threw things back at him to defend myself. Once I picked up my shoe and threw it at him. When he ducked, the shoe went straight through the window, breaking it. Other times, I would pick up Mom's hairbrush and throw it at him. Mom was furious when she had to replace her hairbrush several times and also replace the window.

She would start shouting, "I can't have anything nice in this house because of you kids!" while running after us with her big plank of wood.

Mom was so fed up with our fighting that she made us both bend over behind the couch to spank us. She would make us kids bend over right where Dad was watching TV. I wondered if she did it on purpose to disturb him. Mom whipped us with her thick piece of wood. While we screamed and cried, Dad shouted at us, "Shut up you morons, I'm trying to watch the news!"

If we got in front of the TV while Dad was watching after a long hard day of work, he would shout again, "I'll be damned; I can't watch the TV for these morons!" I always wondered if he really thought we were morons.

I only remember him whipping me once in my entire life; he made me pull my pants down for that whipping. The only time I saw him give Billy a whipping was when he chased him through the yard. I can't even remember what we did to deserve those whippings.

Dad enjoyed watching movies and would often borrow movies from the next-door neighbor. One day Mom was furious when the lady from next door came over to collect her movies. She was dressed in spandex showing off all her curves.

Mom wasn't going to take anything from this woman. She curled her lip and raised her hand saying, "You better get your skinny, slutty a** away from this house!" Then she knocked her out, sending her flat on the ground with a bloody nose.

I was old enough to know that Mom must have been suspicious of her and Dad messing around. Dad wasn't happy with Mom after she knocked out the neighbor lady. From that time on, Mom and Dad didn't get along anymore. As a child, I was heartbroken.

3

Dad was choking Mom and pushing her up against the wall as I walked into the living room. He was saying, "You little b****, I will kill your crazy a**!"

I started crying not knowing why Dad wanted to choke Mom. "Mommy!" I cried, as I felt panicked and wanted my father to stop. "Just go to your room, Sissy, it's okay!" Mom always called me Sissy or Crystola, which had always made me feel good; but this time it didn't make the pain go away.

Not long after that, we came home from school and saw that Mom had tossed all of the food from the fridge around the kitchen. She was obviously angry and upset because her face was red from all her crying. For some reason, she had even taken pictures of the food. Maybe she wanted to use it against Dad, but I wondered how that would work because it looked as if she was the one that threw the food around. Or maybe Dad did it and she was just trying to put the things back in the fridge. I never did find out.

Mom packed up and said we were leaving for good. Our parents looked at us and said, "Who do you want to live with?"

That question pierced my heart like a knife. How could I choose one parent over the other? A child wants to be able to live with both of their parents.

"Mommy, I want to live with you!" I said, while Billy said, "I want to live with my dad!"

Mom said, "The both of you are going to live with me, I'll be damned if I let him take my children from me!"

That was the end of our happy little family. Mom took us to a friend's house to stay for awhile and our parents officially separated. They divorced when I was just nine years old and Billy was eleven. There must have been more reasons for their separation, but that's how I remember it taking place.

When it was time to go before the Judge in the Courthouse, the battle started. They had to decide who got custody of us children and who got all of the things that Dad worked for and bought with his money. It should have been Mom and Dad who went before the Judge since they were the ones that wanted to be separated, but they decided to take us with them through the battle, using us as weapons.

Mom would say, "Your father is a useless man that cheats on his wife and he is a pathological liar!"

Dad would say, "Your Mom is crazy; don't listen to anything she says!"

That is just a glimpse of what they used to say about each other putting negative images into our heads. The war between them continued on for years.

Eventually the courts agreed to give Mom custody of us kids with visitation rights to Dad on the weekends. We would meet Dad at the Courthouse parking lot every other Friday. I can remember eagerly waiting for my Dad to show up, so that we could spend the weekend with him. Sometimes he wouldn't show up, and I would cry while Mom tried her best to console me.

"I just want to see Daddy!" I cried.

Mom looked at me saying, "Why do you allow him to hurt you? Forget about him because he couldn't care less about you!" But he was my father and there was no way that I could forget about him. I wanted to spend time with him and to know that he cared for me and loved me.

Dad was required to pay $50 a week for child support and was allowed to keep all of the assets. Mom packed up all our clothes and everything in our bedrooms and nothing else. She managed to get an old red car from somewhere and negotiated with a friend in the neighborhood for some land and a two-bedroom trailer that we could live in. This was a big change from the huge house we used to live in with Dad. Billy and I would now have to share a room. Our new house was just five houses down the road from Dad. Mom said that she didn't want us to have to change schools, so she chose not to move us out of the district.

On our way to school in the mornings, we would ask Mom for fifty cents to buy a can drink. Mom said, "I can't afford for you two to be fifty-centing me every day, especially after your Dad left me with less than a dollar." I couldn't wait to get to school to eat breakfast, a delicious hot doughnut with a small carton of chocolate milk. Mom couldn't afford to pay for our school lunches, so we ate for free.

I later figured Dad didn't let her take one of his cars because he was making payments on it and he knew Mom may not be able to afford the payments. Dad continued to live in the family house for several years after the divorce.

Mom started working at the Post Office as a janitor and she cleaned peoples' houses to make extra money. She tried her best to take care of Billy and me. She would do anything to make an extra dollar, even if it meant that she would collect aluminum cans from the streets to exchange them for cash.

Many times the lack of funds overwhelmed my mother. I saw her lying on her back on the bed with her feet dangling off, while she cried and wished that all the stress could go away. Sometimes I would go with Mom to town while she ran her errands. We would stop at the gas station and she would write a check to pay for the gas in the car, a pack of cigarettes, and get us something to eat. Instead of writing the check for the exact total of what she had bought, she would write it for an extra amount, so that she could get cash back from the store. Then we would pull up to the bank and she would deposit the cash in the bank to cover a check that she wrote a few days earlier. Then we were off to another store to repeat the same thing.

Mom said, "I'm in the hole and I'm playing catch up!"

4

Our lives had changed dramatically. Mom stopped going to church, our friends no longer came to our house, and she no longer sewed clothes for us after the divorce. That was okay because kids in school would sometimes make fun of us for the clothes we wore. Mom never bought new clothes for us though; she went to yard sales to find them. The kids in school made fun of us anyway, since our clothes were obviously not new. I was not considered popular since I didn't wear the most fashionable clothes. That caused me to place value on material things instead of people.

My grades dropped drastically. My teacher, Mrs. Tarver, was concerned because I had made straight A's in school before our parents divorced.

Sometimes I would see the UPS man delivering packages to our school. Every time I saw him, I would say, "Do you know James? He works at UPS. Please tell him that his daughter said 'Hi' and she loves him." I yearned to have my father in my life.

Mom changed into a different person right after the divorce. I guess it was the best way that she knew how to deal with the pain of separating from her husband of twelve years. She started going out to clubs and leaving us home alone at night. Her favorite club was GiGi's in Little Rock, Arkansas.

She came home one night and said, "Here, I got you a t-shirt!"

"Thanks Mom!" I said, and went in my room to try it on. It was purple with a Playboy bunny on it.

Billy often cooked for us. One time while frying bacon, he accidentally poured the hot grease on his arm. Nearly all the skin on his lower arm was bubbling. His friend said "Put some mustard on it to make it feel better!" But when he did that, Billy screamed in more pain. Mustard obviously was not the trick to make it feel better. We ate a lot of bacon sandwiches or cinnamon toast. I can remember being so hungry one time and having nothing in the kitchen except for bread, so I ate about 10 slices of bread with cinnamon.

Mom came home with a man one day and called him her boyfriend. She seemed to be happy to have met someone. Eventually she said that they were getting married and they bought a new double-wide trailer. It had three bedrooms and two bathrooms, so Billy and I would each have our own bedroom again and a bathroom to share. I could tell that my mother was excited to get a new house and a new husband. We never attended a wedding or saw any pictures of their wedding even though they said they were married.

I thought, "Well, maybe Mom will stop leaving us at home alone at night now and we can have a normal life again!"

Our stepfather's name was Bob and he worked as an automotive painter. So our biological father fixed cars while our stepfather painted them.

Bob was a bit different from our dad; he cooked soups with beer and drank alcohol often. I remember him frequently peeing on the bush in the front of the house and that it was always greener than the rest.

My Dad never drank alcohol; or if he did, I don't remember it. Bob smoked marijuana in the car while Mom and I were with him. Once, as we were driving, I was eating a bag of potato chips, and I started feeling nauseated. "Mom, I don't feel so well!"

"Honey, what's wrong?" she said.

I didn't know what to tell her although I knew it was the smell of the joint that was making me sick. I shouted, "Mom, I am about to puke!" Before she had enough time to pull over, I had already thrown up in the back seat of the car.

Mom didn't like it that Bob drank and smoked marijuana, but he did it anyway. I wondered why she married him in the first place. If he did those things when she met him, she must have thought she could change him once they got married. I never knew my mother to be a heavy drinker or drug user, but she did smoke a pack of cigarettes a day. While I didn't see her drink much, she had a huge container in the living room where she brewed wine.

I would often spend time with my stepfather's brother and his wife; their names were Charles and Rhonda Price. They pretty much adopted me even though I only spent weekends there. I enjoyed staying with them, even if they had no other kids for me to play with. They showed me the love that I needed as a child, and it gave me comfort. They took me to the zoo, taught me how to ride a horse, and Rhonda took me along with her when she went shopping. We also cooked together, something that my mother did not do. Charles was a father figure to me since my own father was no longer in the picture. I enjoyed helping Rhonda with laundry and cleaning the house.

I knew that they thought I was beautiful, smart, strong and a good kid. I think I also filled a void for them because they didn't have a daughter or a child together. Charles had children with his first wife. They were the only family that seemed to have it together and seemed normal. They lived in Little Rock, which was about a thirty-minute drive from our house.

My stepfather's uncle started spending more time with us in our house. He worked at a cookie company in Little Rock. One day he came to our house with a truckload of cookies that were rejected by the company. They were not wrapped and were all the same type. Mom was happy to get so many cookies, as if we could eat the cookies as a meal. I had never seen so many cookies in my life.

While Mom had found a new husband, Dad had also met someone and they got married.

"I want you to meet someone," Dad said as he took us to his friend's house. He pulled up in the driveway and a woman came out of the house. We all got out of the car and walked up to her. "Kids, meet Dorothy!"

"Hi Dorothy!" we said.

She greeted us as she went over to her car to get some candy for us. From that day on, Dad and Dorothy were together and saw each other frequently. Dad didn't seem to waste time finding someone new, because I remembered seeing him with her before the divorce was even final. He soon married her.

She had also been married before she married my father. We never attended a wedding for them either or saw any wedding pictures. I accepted her as my stepmother and enjoyed being with her.

Dorothy lived in Jacksonville, Arkansas, and had her own house. I would help her clean the house when Dad took us to visit before they got married, and she would give me money for helping. She always kept a clean house, just like my mother. There was something about Dorothy that I just loved, and I wished that she could be my mother. I wrote about that in my journal in school; but then my Mom found my journal and read it.

Mom came to me saying, "So, you want her to be your mother?

Then carry your a** down there and live with her because I don't give a s***!" I know I must have broken my mother's heart, and it hurts me today thinking about how it must have made her feel.

Mom and Dorothy didn't get along at all; occasionally they would get into an argument. Mom drove five houses down the road to where Dad and Dorothy lived to tell her how she felt about her. Dorothy responded by breaking Mom's windshield.

Mom told us to steal some of the beef that was in Dad's freezer for us to eat. He still got a huge amount of beef from his parents every year. She was no longer entitled to the meat, but still needed it to feed her children.

Mom's marriage with Bob didn't last long and they started arguing much like she and Dad had done. Thankfully, I never saw Bob choke our mother, though she later told me that he did try to choke her once. I don't know what it was with men choking my mother. At least this time we didn't have to go through the divorce process to decide who got custody of the children and the things that Mom owned. We belonged to Mom and Bob didn't own anything.

After they divorced, Mom was back to clubbing again. I guess she was searching for her next husband. It was too bad she didn't learn that there were better places to find a husband than inside a bar. If a woman looks for love in a bar, she should know what type of man she will find. But my mother was searching for someone to love her, someone that she could spend the rest of her life with.

During this period of time Mom started coming home drunk with her friends. I slept in the living room during those cold nights to keep warm by the fireplace because she couldn't afford to pay for central heat.

One night I was awakened by a commotion outside. It was Mom and her partying friends. One of them puked and made all kinds of noise. Mom told him, "Shut your drunken a** up, my kids is sleeping! You can't hold down your liquor for nothing!" The friend only laughed and squirmed in the chair. The friend then fell asleep in the living room.

Mom said, "Billy, you and your sister go to your room!"

Late one lonely night, Mom brought yet another man home with her. He was missing an eye because he had gotten into a fight at a bar and somebody threw a beer bottle at him. He was tall and skinny with curly black hair. Dennis started living with us from time to time. One day Mom went to work when we were out of school for the summer, so we were home alone. Billy and I, along with Billy's friend, and a little boy that the friend was babysitting, were the only people home. Dennis came down the long dirt driveway with a washing machine in the back of his pickup truck. He came to the door and asked, "Where's your mother?"

We told him, "She went to work."

Billy said, "My friend and I are going down the road and will be back soon; this kid is going to stay here with you, Crystal!"

Shortly after they left, Dennis asked me, "Do you have any aloe vera?"

There wasn't any in my mother's bedroom, so I came out of the room saying, "I can't find any," while wondering what he wanted to do with it.

He said, "Go and check again."

As I entered the room once more, he followed me and closed the door. Then he put his arm around me and held a knife at my neck. I was just 13 years old, and I thought he felt like he needed protection from me. My heart started racing. I didn't understand what he wanted to do. After all, I was doing what he asked by looking for the aloe vera. He said, "Sit down on the bed and keep your mouth shut!"

"What do you want? Why are you doing this to me?" I started crying. He locked the door and came over to me. "It's okay, don't cry! Take your shirt off!" he commanded.

I looked at him and said, "I don't have any breasts."

He said, "That's okay, they'll grow."

I was reluctant to take my shirt off, so he took it off for me. I wondered what he could possibly want with me as a child. He made me do horrific things and we were in the bedroom for what seemed like hours while the little boy was in the living room all by himself and my brother was gone. I wanted to shout at the boy and tell him to go get help; but Dennis said to me, "I will kill you if you tell anyone about this. If they catch me, I will send someone else to come and kill you!"

Trying to distract him, I kept saying, "My mom is going to be home soon and we need to get out of her bedroom," hoping that he would just stop and let me go. I cried so much that when I looked up at him, he appeared to have one eye in the middle of his face and he looked like a frightening creature to me. After all he did have only one eye, and he had proved that he was a frightening man.

Finally I said, "I need to go to the bathroom." There was a bathroom in Mom's bedroom, and I ran inside and locked the door behind me—he had removed all my clothes. I didn't really have to use the bathroom; I just wanted to escape from him.

Soon he started pounding on the door. "What are you doing in there? You better open this door!"

I was trying to cut the screen on the window thinking that I could crawl out and run to get help. The window was too small for me to fit through; and then I realized that if I succeeded, I would be going outside naked. I just wanted to close my eyes and wake up in a safe place.

He must have realized what I was doing because he went outside to the window and threatened me, "You better open that door unless you want me to kill you!"

I truly thought he might kill me, and he was trying to scare me into opening the door. So I gave up and opened it. He said, "Put your clothes back on," and he let me go.

As I walked out of the bedroom, the little boy was still in the living room and I had no idea what to say to him or how to act. I couldn't wait to run away and tell somebody what had just happened to me. We went outside to ride our bikes; and I whispered, "Something terrible just happened to me and we have to get away."

He looked at me and asked, "What happened?"

"That man molested me!"

"What does that mean?"

"It means something very bad happened to me! Let's act as if we are just riding our bikes up and down the driveway and then we'll make a run for it."

So we rode our bicycles away from the house down the long driveway. When I was sure he could no longer see us down by the road, I raced to my dad's house. I was thankful Mom had made the decision not to move too far from Dad; I was sure he would help me. Dad slept in the daytime because he worked at night, so I knew it wouldn't do any good to go to the front door. His bedroom window was too high for me to reach; and as I stood at the window, I thought to myself, *How will I ever wake him up so that I can tell him what that man just did to his daughter?* I didn't think to throw a rock or a stick at the window to wake him up. I just couldn't think straight. I was confused. I just wanted to tell someone. I have always wondered how he would have handled the situation, or if he would have even cared what happened to me if I had been able to wake him and tell him.

Since I couldn't figure out what to do, I left there and went to the house of friends that lived across the road from Dad—friends that I had played with often. One of the girls came to answer my knock at the door.

"Something very bad has just happened! Please, call the police for me!" I said as I tried hard to hold back my tears.

"Why? What happened to you? Who is that boy with you?"

She called her older sister to the door, but she said, "Sorry, our parents said we can't have any friends over when they are not at home! Go to your Dad's house!"

"My dad is sleeping! Don't worry; I will go to Uncle Bill's house,"

Uncle Bill was an old man that lived down the road. He was a good friend of my parents from the time I was a small girl. I told him what happened even though it was extremely embarrassing to talk about it. He promptly called the police.

I never knew before that day that there was an undercover cop who lived next door to Dad, and he came right over. Soon a detective drove up with my Mom in the car and started asking me questions.

Mom didn't run to me or hug me, even though she must have known what had happened to me since the detective brought her along. As I think back on that day, it seems that a normal mother would have tried to offer comfort. I now think that my mother probably felt so much guilt that she didn't know how to deal with it. I was taken to the hospital for an examination and the detective kept asking me all kinds of questions about what happened.

Mom was told to go to her home where Dennis was and act as if nothing had happened so that the police could move in and make an arrest. It was my dad's neighbor, the undercover cop, who arrested Dennis and took him to jail. He eventually served seven years in the state penitentiary.

I went to stay with one of Mom's friends. Her daughter and I were close in age and were good friends. I stayed with them for a few weeks and the social worker came to visit me often to talk about what happened. She brought me a teddy bear in an attempt to make me feel better.

Although I desperately needed my parents, they were still not around for me. My father never once discussed the incident with me. After all, what could he say? I suppose it was a subject too painful to discuss, so nobody uttered a word. My mom somehow understood how uncomfortable I became around older men. She would often ask me if I was okay or if I was comfortable.

When it was time to go back to school after the summer was over, I thought, *Wow, what a summer vacation!*

As I went back to school, everybody seemed to know about what had happened to me. I hung my head down in shame. One of my classmates came to me and said with a sad look on her face, "Sorry for what happened." I wondered how my fellow classmates knew about it. Then I learned that the incident had been reported in the newspaper. Although the reporter did not include my name, information like that spreads easily in such a small town and it was apparently fodder for the rumor mill.

Billy's friend came to me saying, "Aloe vera," as he chuckled.

The pain inside me was excruciating, yet I would laugh with him as I tried to hide my pain. My brother betrayed me and must have told his friend the details of what happened.

Mom wrote to Dennis while he was in prison and told me that I should also write to him. Inside, my heart was crying, *Mom, why are you doing this to me? Why are you writing to the man that abused your daughter?* To please my mother, I wrote him a letter: "Dear Dennis, Mom said I should write you a letter, so that's what I am doing now. I don't understand why you did that to me. Regardless of why you did it, I will try to forgive you!"

He wrote back, "I am so sorry for what I did to you and I hope that you can forgive me. I have some things that I need to deal with from my childhood."

After writing to tell him that I forgave him, I was truly relieved of the resentment I felt towards him. However, that didn't mean there was no psychological scar in my life. It was an odd moment for me, writing to the person who violated me and who exposed me to a world that I, as a 13-year-old, had been totally unaware.

A short while later, we were driving home and Mom said, "I want you to meet someone real quick." As we drove up to a house, Mom said, "I want you to meet a woman that was also abused by Dennis. They were about to get married and he raped her!"

As we stood on the front porch, I just knew the woman had to think something was wrong with my mother who thought it was important to introduce her daughter to a grown woman that was abused by the same person that abused me. What an awkward moment for both of us! I just wanted my pain to go away and to get on with my life, but my mother was probably trying to deal with it the best way she knew how. I couldn't understand my mother's behavior, but I knew it was not normal.

Mom was angry with me and would sometimes shout at me saying,

"It's your fault because you climbed in the bed with him and you were always walking around in your nightgown."

I thought, *Really? So an innocent 13-year-old girl shouldn't be wearing her nightgown in her own house, especially when her mom was bringing different men home?* But I said nothing.

I wept in my room, not understanding why my mother would blame me. Maybe she felt guilty for leaving me without supervision and allowing that useless man to come to our house. A part of me wondered if I did something to provoke him. I began to wonder if it was my fault; but I forgave my mom in my heart because I knew it was not entirely her fault. Even if it was, I forgave her. I knew that deep down it must have hurt her a lot and she just didn't know how to deal with what had happened.

As Billy and I entered our adolescent years, our behaviors began to change. Mom didn't know how to deal with us, so she let us do what we wanted as long as we didn't bother her. She made sure we had food to eat, clothes on our backs, and that we got up every morning for school. She did the best she knew how, but she was hampered by the way she was raised and by the fact that she was a single parent. One day Mom came from work and noticed that the house had holes on two sides of the living room. "What in the h*** happened there?" she shouted.

Billy explained, "Uh, I was shooting my gun and the bullet ricocheted and hit the house!"

"I've not even finished paying for this house and you're busy destroying it! Get me my stick!" she yelled. Mom had a big thick piece of wood that she used to beat us. Sometimes she would beat us until we had bruises that turned blue or purple.

When Billy was about to turn 16 years old, he told Mom he wanted to have a big party. She agreed and allowed him to invite all his friends and even bought kegs of beer for him. Billy was excited to have a mom that would let him have so much fun with his friends. He didn't know how she was harming us.

The party was held on a Friday night. I was not involved in the party and was trying to sleep because I had Saturday school the next morning. Two of the party-goers (a boy and a girl) came into the room where I was sleeping. They noticed that I was in there, so they quickly left. The party went on for a long time that night.

Saturday school was a punishment given by the principal of our school to those who skipped school. I had started skipping school and lost interest in my education. Nobody spoke to me about the importance of learning. Saturday school always took place at Benton Public School, which was in a town close to Bauxite. We had to spend time in the cafeteria with students from other area schools who were also being punished.

My friends and I skipped school often to do nothing in particular. I started disrespecting my teachers, goofing off in class, never doing assignments or homework, and sleeping in class. My home life was affecting my behavior. Mom never encouraged me to do my homework or study to get good grades. She couldn't help me with my homework at all since she had quit school so young. She would often ask me how to spell words. Ironically, she enjoyed writing poems and often framed them to sell.

We didn't see much of our father and it affected me tremendously. My father was dedicated to paying child support and buying Christmas gifts for us; but he didn't know how to be a father—to show that he cared, to call and say, "Hi, I love you," or ask, "How are you doing?" He didn't know how to spend quality time with us as a father. I wrote long letters to my dad trying to tell him how I felt, but he didn't respond.

In an attempt to get my parents' attention I often cried and said, "I hate my life and I am going to end it by killing myself." That made matters worse because Mom starting taking me to see a counselor thinking that she could figure out what was wrong with me. I didn't need a counselor; I needed my mother and father to love me and to give me a structured life. I thought by making those claims that I could get their attention. I never actually tried to kill myself; it was just my way of expressing how miserable I felt inside, even though at times I did feel like dying and wished that my life would end.

Mom let me stay overnight with my best friend Cheryll. At her house I watched *The Silence of the Lambs* and rode her grandpa's go-cart. I felt happy to be having fun again like a child and forgot for a time about my life at home. One time when Cheryll spent the night with me at my father's house, my stepmother made hamburgers and cheese dip for us—my favorite.

Then a new girl named Melinda came to school. Now the three of us spent time in each other's homes. Melinda's sister-in-law drank alcohol and she let us drink. We thought it was a cool thing to do. She also taught us how to shoplift at Walmart. Mom asked about various items I brought home: "Where did you get that from?" or "Who bought that for you?" I told her that Melinda's sister-in-law stole it for us. At first, she had a problem with the thefts, until she realized that it was an opportunity for her to get things too. From that point on, she told me what items I should steal for her.

So now, at the age of fifteen, I was failing in school and had become a thief. I had no direction in life.

Eventually I got caught stealing at Walmart and a detective called Mom. At that point she decided that I shouldn't hang around Melinda and her family anymore.

I still saw Cheryll often; and once when she came to spend the night with me at my mom's house, Billy and his friends were outside my bedroom window smoking marijuana. Billy knocked on the window and said, "Come on out and smoke with us!" I had never smoked marijuana before, but I had smelled it and had seen it because of my mother's husband smoking it in the car that day a few years earlier. Billy taught me how to smoke. "Just hold it like this and inhale it!" he said as he demonstrated for me. As I tried to inhale, I choked and coughed, and tried to catch my breath. I was afraid they would make fun of me if I didn't smoke with them, so I continued trying. I didn't enjoy it and couldn't understand the point of it.

Our school had a tradition of letting out classes for "deer day." That was the day when school closed for deer hunting. Cheryll had a friend who went to Bryant Public School, a school which didn't observe that practice; so we formulated a plan to get her friend out of school. We said, "Let's make a bomb threat to the school and then they will get out for the day, too!" We looked up the number in the phone book and called them.

Disguising my voice, I said, "There is a bomb in your school and you better get out!"

I don't know why I didn't let Cheryll make the call, but it was so much fun at the time. Our school would often get calls from someone with the threat of a bomb, but never once was there a bomb in our school. So, that's where the idea came from.

A short time later, two detectives pulled into the driveway with Mom in the car. This time Mom had a greater reaction to what had happened, unlike the last time she rode in the car with the detective because of me. She was shocked and disappointed.

As they were coming down the driveway, we decided to pretend we were sleeping to look innocent, thinking that they would never know. But the police had traced the phone call and arrived at our house just a few minutes after we made the phone call. They did not put us in jail since we were under age, but I was placed on probation and had to see a judge.

Once again I was placed in Saturday school.

At the age of 15, I met a boy at Saturday school. He sat down beside me and said, "What's your name?"

"Crystal, what's yours?"

"My name is Randy, but some people call me Two!" he replied. "What did you do to get Saturday school?"

"I got caught skipping school."

We had so much in common and exchanged phone numbers. We called each other often. He told me that I was beautiful and that made me feel like I was soaring. I couldn't remember anybody ever telling me that before. My self-esteem was very low due to all I had been through. I felt like fireworks were going off.

One day as I was talking to Randy on the phone, Mom walked in. She said, "Is that a nigger you're talking to? You better get off that d*** phone right this minute!" I had never heard that word before; but I figured a nigger must be a black person.

Billy had gotten his first job at the same place where Randy worked and had overheard Randy talking about a girl named Crystal, so he came home and told Mom. I wondered why Billy thought it was a problem and felt like he needed to tell Mom that Randy was black. I didn't see any problem with it. I saw him as a human being just like the rest of us. Dad called the house and asked to speak to me. As I put the receiver to my ear, I was afraid of what my father would say to me.

Dad said, "Crystal, if you don't stop talking to that nigger, then I will disown you!" That was all that he had to say.

Well, I wasn't the idiot that everybody thought I was. I knew it was downright absurd that my mother and father were so nonchalant about anything that happened in my life before, and suddenly they wanted to have a say about my life just because I was talking to a black boy on the phone. It didn't matter to them that they hurt me when they divorced, or when Mom's boyfriend abused me.

They never took the time to tell me about my education or any other life skills. I thought, *So you mean it is okay for you to blame me for your useless boyfriend, but it's not okay to speak to a black boy on the phone just because of his skin color?"* That was like pouring gasoline on a fire. I was furious that they were being so ridiculous and that they wanted to cut me off from the only person that made me feel happy. I thought, *These white people that I grew up with my entire life didn't like black people only because of their skin color and not because of anything that they did!*

I remembered that my Dad had brought a black man he worked with to our house when our parents were married, but I never once thought that my parents had racial biases. Billy shook the man's hand, and then looked at his own hand to see if it had turned black. Everybody just laughed it off as childish curiosity. I knew that our Dad didn't want us to watch Michael Jackson or Michael Jordan on TV, but it never dawned on me that it was because they were black.

My friends at school even rejected me simply because the boy I was talking to on the phone was black. Once again, everybody in the school knew about my personal life. I had entered into a whole new world that I didn't understand. Nobody in my school wanted anything to do with me anymore except for the only biracial girl in the school, Kaylee, my friend from elementary school. When I sat down in class, the other kids, including my own brother, would move away from me saying, "Nigger Lover." They looked at me in disgust. Obviously these kids' parents had already taught them that black people were different from white people.

They had brainwashed these kids instead of teaching them to love and respect people regardless of their skin color. I didn't know what they had told their children, but I knew it wasn't right. I hated going to school.

I cried and begged my Mom, "Please don't make me go back to that school!"

I could see in her eyes for the first time that she felt pity for me. I wanted her to let me go to school in Benton because that was where the black people went to school, even though I didn't dare tell her that was the reason. I thought that people there would be less likely to reject me since there were many blacks in the school. There may have been more racists as well, but at least it would be controlled since they were hesitant to show their bigotry in front of the black people. Mom refused and said she did not want me to switch schools because she would have to take me to school and pick me up every day.

When I was 16, I started working at McDonalds. I loved working there because I could be around black people. I started hanging out with some of the friends I met there and then Mom made me quit my job when she found out that some of them were black.

I became rebellious and ran away from home. I no longer wanted to live with these people that didn't want me to be friends with someone because of their skin color. I completely lost interest in school.

Randy lived on "The Hill," an area in Benton where all of the black people lived, separated from the white people. I went to visit Randy there; and once again, I was amazed that even these people separated themselves from the whites and lived in an area designated strictly for black people. Since the black people were the only ones who didn't reject me, I spent time with them because they obviously didn't have a problem with discrimination like my family and the people in my school.

Once again I realized I was living in a confused world. I made up my mind that I didn't like white people, even though I am white. In a teenage identity crisis, I decided I wanted to be like black people. I now knew how it felt to be rejected and I learned how black people were routinely rejected for their skin color

Since I was on juvenile probation, I got into more trouble when I ran away from home. Mom called the police and they found me and took me back home. During our next court date, Mom told the Judge that I ran away from home, and she asked if there was a residence where I could be placed. The Judge ordered that I be sent to a nearby center for troubled teens called Rivendell. I thought it was funny and told my Mom, "It looks like now you will be locking me up with black people and I will no longer have to run away to be with them." I was amazed at how much energy they put into making sure I didn't associate with black people. Ironically, at one point my mother was okay with me having a friend who was bi-racial and also allowed my brother's black friend live with us. Our parents just did not want us to be more than friends with a black person.

The Judge did not want to send me to Rivendell simply because he thought I shouldn't be with a black boy, but he saw that I needed some direction in my life. That was something my parents couldn't quite figure out. The Judge didn't question how my parents were raising me, but surely he thought they were doing something wrong. The more my parents pressed the issue of my not mixing with the black people, the more I wanted to be with them.

Mom told me, "It says in the Bible that blacks and whites shouldn't mix."

"Show me where in the Bible it says that."

"I can't remember which part of the Bible; I will have to look it up!" she replied.

So instead of teaching me about God's love and how he wants us to show love to all people, she lied and tried to make me think that God didn't approve of it either. I thought if God didn't intend for us to mix races or ethnicity, then he would have made us all alike. There is not one verse in the entire Bible that says that a white woman should not marry a black man or vice versa. My parents would have preferred for me to be gay, or to be with a man that beat me, as long as they were white.

I did end up going to Rivendell and spent several months there. I talked to people about my problems and I attended classes. There I was finally able to make up for all of the school work that I had previously missed. One of the youth workers told me to write about my feelings towards my father, so I did. It helped to express how I felt rejected by him and it felt good that someone seemed to care. One of our close neighbors worked there and it was always pleasant to see a familiar face. Mom visited me occasionally. I cried, telling her, "I am ready to go home." The concerned look on her face made me realize that she really did love me.

5

When I was released from Rivendell, I went back to live with Mom. It felt good to be back at home where I could have freedom to take a bath or eat when I wanted. That didn't last long, however. One day I asked Mom, "Can I go to the movies tonight?" "It depends on who you are going to the movies with. If you're planning on going with a bunch of niggers, then you can forget it!" "I'm going with Kaylee."

"H*** no, you're not going with Kaylee! I don't want any nigger babies walking around here!"

"Kaylee has white friends, Mom! Plus, nobody is having any babies!" I pleaded.

"You heard what I said, d*** it."

I wasn't going to take "no" for an answer. I knew Mom didn't want me to go with Kaylee because she was black. Mom kept the phone in her bedroom and locked the door to prevent me having any contact with people. One time when she left the door open, I snuck in and called Kaylee and asked her to pick me up at the end of my driveway.

Mom thought she could stop me from hanging out with black people, but as soon as I got to school I plotted how I would make it to The Hill to meet up with Karl. I had met him at the movies the night I sneaked out of the house. Soon I ran away from home every weekend to see him.

I continually ran away from home for nearly two years. Once I sneaked out my bedroom window and came back home to find Mom outside the front door. She was holding her fist up at me. "You are not coming back in this house through the door. You'd better climb back through that window!" So I climbed through the window that led to my bedroom.

Karl hid me in his bedroom sometimes and his sisters would sneak food in for me. I thought I had my first love. His mother invited me to go to church with them on The Hill. I felt so comfortable being surrounded by black people who didn't reject me.

One time Karl's mother caught me inside his bedroom. She was big enough to block the entrance to the door, so she just stood there to make sure that I didn't escape.

"Get me the phone, Stephanie!" she told Karl's sister. And then to the police on the phone she said, "I have a teenage runaway in my house. Come and get her!"

There wasn't much that the police could do, so they called my Mom to come and pick me up. My mother was so stressed over dealing with my behavior and she had no solution to my rebellion other than sending me away again. However, she was never afraid to give me a good beating.

When we got home this time, she grabbed my hair and pulled me through the house in pure frustration. I was soon on my way to the next home for troubled teens. I stayed in four different places that took in juvenile delinquents—children like me that had missed the road and didn't have any direction in their lives, children that were searching for someone to love them and nurture them. Since there was only one center for troubled teens in our area, Mom started searching in other cities. She sent me to Sherwood, Batesville, and Newport, Arkansas.

Finally she sent me to live with my cousin's ex-boyfriend that lived in Springdale. He lived in a fancy house and worked as a contractor who built houses. He took me to the mall and bought me new clothes. Mom wasn't afraid that another man could molest me. I was just a headache in her life and she wanted me to go away.

My cousin's ex-boyfriend didn't live far from the rest of the family on my mother's side in Fayetteville. I met up with a cousin who was four years older than me and who had given birth to a bi-racial child at the age of sixteen. I wanted to surround myself with her family because her mother and father didn't seem to be racists. My aunt seemed to be the sweetest person, never judging me for my decision. Rather, she would show how she cared. I wanted to live with them, but my mother refused because she knew her sister accepted black people. That frightened my mom. I had no choice but to go back home with my mom.

All the time I had been living elsewhere, Mom had a pen pal who was in prison. His name was Danny and they exchanged letters frequently. The picture she had in her room showed him in his prison uniform. She decided to go and meet him at the prison; and after visiting him frequently, she became engaged to him.

My mother was getting married to a man who was in prison for raping a woman. Although he told my Mom that he was not guilty, I was amazed and incredibly hurt by her decision.

I asked myself, "How can my mother marry a rapist after what her boyfriend did to me?"

This time I saw pictures of their wedding even though I didn't attend. It was held in the prison chapel. Mom wore a white dress while her husband wore his white prison uniform. I went with her to the prison a few times in Calico Rock or Hope, wherever he was serving his time. As we passed through security and went to the waiting room, Mom talked about some of the other men in the prison that were sitting and waiting for their visitors.

Mom said, "You know, Danny knows some of these men in here. He could introduce to you one and you could start writing to him!"

"I think I will pass on that, Mom!" I said.

My mother introduced me to one of her husband's friends in prison hoping that I would be interested in him. She thought it was better for me to be with a white man in prison than to be with someone who was black. I thought, *That's some backward thinking.*

Mom and Danny were married for several years and she became obsessed with recording their every conversation. She had a dresser full of recorded tapes. Mom talked about how important it was to keep records and to not throw away receipts for documentation purposes, but I thought she was being a little extreme.

One day I walked into the room and she was listening to one of her taped conversations.

"Mom, what are you doing?" I said with my nose curled up.

"Leave me the h*** alone, it is none of your d*** business what I'm doing!" she shouted.

"Mom, you are weird!"

"I don't care what you think about me, now get the h*** out of my room!" she said, slamming the door and locking it.

Mom's new husband didn't choke her; I suppose it would have been difficult to do so since he was in prison. This was my mother's fourth marriage, because she had been married before she married my father.

After a few years Mom and Danny divorced. Then Mom went to court to sue him for all she had spent on gas driving to see him every weekend and for all of the collect phone calls that she accepted from him.

I believe Mom was desperate for someone to love her, something that we all search for in life. Everybody wants to be loved and appreciated. She just didn't realize she was searching for companionship in the wrong places. I am not sure why her marriages didn't last, most likely because the marriage was not centered on God. Mom often sent her boyfriends or husbands away from the house in anger saying, "Get your lazy a** out of my house and don't ever come back!"

I now feel sure she had her own childhood story. Her behaviors must have been linked to her past.

My Grandmother was married several times. Her one son and five daughters had three different fathers. My mother grew up thinking that her stepfather was her biological father until a man appeared at the door one day when she was a teenager and told her that he was her real father. I remember going to her father's place to see him once. He lived in a camper, was very poor, and owned lots of rabbits. My aunt said that their mother was very mean to my mom. Her older sister took care of her as a child and they lived in poverty themselves. During the time of my parents' divorce, Mom learned through a phone call that her father had died in a tractor accident. She cried in her bedroom and tried to console herself by listening to "One day at a Time" by Crystal Gale. Even though I only met my grandfather once or twice, I cried too. Mom heard me in the other room and came to comfort me.

My mother told me that she had been sexually abused by one of her mother's husbands. Just as my mom searched for love in the wrong places, so did I. Out of my search for someone to love me, I lost my virginity at a very young age. From that time, my mind and my heart were filled with confusion and hurt. I continued my search to find someone that would love me, only to find out that those boys cared nothing for me and their only thought was to use me. I was confused, hurt, and ignorant. My mother or father had never spoken to me about sex, drugs, alcohol, friends, money, Jesus, education or anything of importance to a teenager. I spent my life trying to figure it out on my own, making one mistake after another. And history was repeating itself.

When my mother was going through the divorce from her latest husband, I plotted how I could make it back to my cousin's house— the cousin she didn't want me to live with. One day when my mother went to take a bath, I took her car and drove back to Fayetteville so that I could live with my aunt and cousin.

While I was driving, I started to change the station on the radio. Suddenly I felt the car going off the road and onto the shoulder. It scared me, so I jerked the wheel causing the car to go in circles. The car ended up on the wrong side of the road right on top of a tree stump, which had prevented the car from falling down a very steep cliff. I should have been dead! In my shock I tried to start the car again, thinking I could just be on my way; but the car was hung up on that stump and could not go anywhere. A police officer happened to be passing by and stopped to help me out of the car. He called a wrecker to come and pull the car out. When the man driving the wrecker showed up dressed in his overalls, he looked at the officer and said in his southern accent, "Was she drunk?"

The police officer replied, "Nope, she ain't drunk!"

I was surprised that the officer didn't put me in jail. I was only 16 years old and had no driver's license. I don't remember what kind of lie I gave him, but he gave me a ride into the nearest town since the accident had taken place in the middle of the Ozark Mountains. I called a friend to pick me up, and I was relieved to make it to my aunt's house.

Living with them made me happy. My cousin and I shared a room, a bed, clothes, perfume, socks, shoes, and everything. We became like sisters and went everywhere together. People often told us that we looked alike; and since our mothers were sisters, there really was a resemblance. When Christmas came, I felt like I had a family, something I hadn't felt in such a long time. They treated me like their daughter; they took care of me and showed me love through both words and actions.

Sometime later, when I was seventeen years old, my father and his wife showed up to visit me. I was so happy to see my father because I always thought he didn't care about or love me. "I want you to come and live with me," he said.

A whole new feeling of excitement rushed through me. I thought my father had disowned me and that he wouldn't ever be a part of my life again. All along I just wanted someone to understand me for who I was and to love me. And now, suddenly, my father came to rescue me and try to give me a good life.

We drove three hours to his house in North Little Rock. I was now a part of his house and a part of his family. I had my own room across from his. They bought me everything I wanted. My stepmom and I would go to the mall shopping together every weekend. She frequently took me to Sonic to get a burger and a slushy. Those times together were special to me. She made my favorite foods and made sure I was happy. She even took me to church a few times.

I met some great friends across the street who were Christians and Dad even approved of them! He knew that they were good people and wouldn't be a bad influence on me. He was also happy that they were not black. I accompanied them to church often and went to their grandma's house after church.

My father continued to prohibit my association with black people. I was not allowed to have any friends over while he was gone, but I disobeyed. I brought my black friends to the house and the neighbors told Dad. When he found out, he was very angry with me. One day when nobody was home, I brought my black friend to my house and into my bedroom. My stepmom came home and heard us talking. She opened the door and said, "Get that black guy out of my d*** house!"

Dad came home from work to deal with me. He didn't hit me, but he called me a nigger b****. I couldn't believe my father had called me that. I didn't ever remember him using such fowl words! He normally held his feelings inside. He told me I was grounded and could not come out of my room. I was hurt, and I retaliated by running away to a friend's house. Another cousin came to pick me up and took me back to Fayetteville. My dad didn't try to bring me back to his house, and soon he and his wife moved away from there. I don't remember receiving one phone call from my father, other than the time that he called me to tell me that he would disown me if I didn't stay away from the blacks. I suppose that is why I spent my entire childhood wondering how he felt about me.

It seemed it was too late for my dad to help me; I had already been through so much in my childhood that it would take great amount of effort to change my behavior. Perhaps my dad didn't have enough energy to deal with my rebellious behavior. He didn't know half of the things that went on while I was living with my mother. Since he was not actively involved, it was impossible for him to know. He didn't understand what happened to me as a child. To him, I was just a teenager who thought I knew everything and wanted to be on my own. He didn't realize that I wanted desperately to be part of a normal family.

It all comes down to one problem: sin; and one solution: raising children in the fear of the Lord, teaching them about God and being a good example, and raising children in a united home instead of a broken home. Parents must realize that it's not about them anymore, it's about their children. Parents need to concentrate on making every possible effort to teach their children and lead them into the right direction. They can't come into a child's life after being uninvolved for many years and expect things to work out without a great deal of effort.

I am grateful that my father tried to help me and show me love at that time in his life. If I had it to do over, I would have stayed with my father and made wiser decisions. I didn't know any better though; I knew absolutely nothing about life. But I can't change the past; I can only look toward the future and make better choices. I do not have to be a product of my past or a product of my parents' past!

Exodus 20:12 says, "Honor your mother and father." I forgive my parents and I refuse to spend a lifetime blaming them for my past. The past is gone and I will never know what caused my parents to make certain decisions in their lives. All I can do is leave it for God to judge while I honor them and respect them. At the same time, I am certain that my perspective of how things turned out is most likely different from theirs.

After studying about social work in my adult life, I began to have a better understanding of why I did the things I did as a child. I was also able to better understand my mother's behavior. Experts say it is more likely for children who grow up in a broken home or have a dysfunctional childhood to have issues while growing up: high school dropout, drug or alcohol addiction, prison, or suicide. I pray I can make a difference in the lives of people who have gone through things similar to what I went through as a child.

Another factor in my dad's life is that he didn't grow up with his own father. His father was away serving in the U.S Navy. When he came home to visit his wife, my grandmother, he found her pregnant. He knew it was not possible that he was the father and he could not deal with the fact of her infidelity. He ran away and no one in the family ever saw him again, heard where he had moved, or knew when he died. At least that is what my mother told me.

My father was physically and verbally abused by his stepfather, and that must have affected his outlook on life. I suppose he tried the best he knew how to be a father, but it doesn't change the fact that I felt like I grew up without a father.

6

When I was seventeen years old, I decided to quit school; and I had no plan for my future. What was I thinking! It's amazing now to realize how my thoughts were childish, not knowing that every choice I made would have a long-lasting affect on me. I never thought about my future; my thoughts never stretched further than where I would find love. I didn't know then that real love begins with Jesus Christ, the one that died on the cross for my sins. I grew up thinking, "What can people do for me?" instead of "What can I do for myself?"

Because of my past experience, I became mistrustful of white men and feared what they might do to me in light of the abuse done to me by my mother's boyfriend. The lack of a secure relationship with my father also affected my outlook. I grew up thinking all men were alike: selfish, abusive deadbeats.

I once saw a father with his daughter in a restaurant having lunch together. I gazed at the two of them, amazed at how this father had a relationship with his daughter, something I had never seen before. I thought all men were the same as my father.

When I was eighteen years old, on November 23, 1998, I met Albert Olaolu Owonubi. It happened when I dialed a wrong phone number. I thought I was calling another boy named Albert, whom I had known many years before. However, Albert Owonubi answered the phone. We talked for a while, and continued to call each other for weeks until we decided to meet.

Albert knocked on the front door of my apartment and I peered through the peephole to see what he looked like. "He's cute!" I told my roommate. He looked so handsome and innocent. I wanted to pick him up and put him in my pocket to keep forever.

As I opened the door, Albert looked at my roommate and me and said, "Which one is Crystal?"

We spent every day together after our first meeting. I shared my life with him. I told him how I had quit school, was abused, was rejected by my father, and how my mother had been married many times. The way he listened to me helped to mend my broken heart. He cared and he gave me a chance. He saw me as a beautiful, determined individual regardless of all the obstacles in my way.

Albert was the only one that truly influenced me to go back to school. He didn't say it just once, but kept encouraging me. He also made me realize how important education is. He was attending the University of Arkansas in Fayetteville, and being with him made me yearn to return to my studies. I wanted to accomplish something with my life.

A few months later I was having a hard time finding another job and I didn't have money to help pay rent. My roommate told me that I should move out of her apartment. I had nowhere to go.

Albert was out of school for the summer, so he told me that I should come and stay with him in the dorm. I stayed there until I found a job and got my own apartment; then he moved in with me. We couldn't stand to be apart from each other, we were so in love! But we were still so young!

We spent hours upon hours talking to each other and spending time together. I felt honored to call him my boyfriend. I took Albert to my aunt's house for Thanksgiving dinner with the extended family and everybody loved him.

Shortly after that, Albert came home one day and found me crying. "I'm pregnant!" I said. I was afraid and nervous.

Albert, like any other man his age, was frightened when he found out that we would be having a baby. "I do not want a baby right now! I think that you should have an abortion!" I cried again in frustration. I had thought all those years of living in pain and rejection was over.

When I told my mom about my pregnancy, she agreed that I should have an abortion. Her reason was different: "I don't want any black grandbabies running around here."

Due to all the pressure, I agreed to have the abortion. My mom paid for me to abort my baby and we went together to the clinic. I can remember walking out of the clinic feeling so dizzy that I could barely stand straight.

Afterward, Albert told me that he didn't want to be with me anymore. I couldn't understand why he wanted to leave me after I had done what he wanted by having an abortion. We still lived together in the apartment, but he would go out at night and I would wait up all night for him to come home. I cried for days and lost a lot of weight. I became depressed after the abortion. I felt betrayed by Albert after thinking that he cared for me and loved me. The truth is that we were just young and ignorant, both of us being only eighteen years old. According to him, he did love me and care for me. He just wasn't ready to be a father, and I wanted to have a baby so that I would finally have someone to love me. Albert wanted to finish his education before having a family.

We fought every day. It hurt me to know he was seeing other women—and I was pregnant again with his baby. I was so sick and tired of being rejected, used, and abused in my life that I could no longer control my emotions. We threw things and broke stuff. Our entire apartment was in shambles. At one point the door to the apartment no longer closed because it had been slammed so many times that the doorknob was falling off and the deadbolt lock was broken.

Eventually Albert moved in with one of his good friends. The house was just a block away from my apartment, so I would go and try to speak to him; but he refused to see me. When I saw him with other women, I would retaliate by trying to fight them.

After losing my apartment yet again, I went back to stay with my cousin, sleeping on her couch every night. One time in the middle of the night when I was about eight months pregnant, I walked from her house across town to Albert's house. He was passed out from either drinking or smoking something. As he came to, he looked up at me in disgust and said, "What do you want?" Albert had totally blocked me out of his mind and it made me feel so hopeless and helpless.

Having nowhere else to go, I was forced to live in a maternity home for pregnant women who had no other options. I stayed there until I was able to get an apartment once again, receiving help from the government and from the maternity home.

I did manage to get a job despite the fact that I was soon to deliver my baby. While on the job, I called Albert to tell him I was having contractions; and he willingly picked me up to take me to the hospital. It was false labor so he took me back to work. When I went into real labor, I was with my half-brother (my father's first son from his wife before he married my mother). My water broke and he rushed me to the hospital, driving fast with his hazard lights on.

Albert came to the hospital to be with me during the birth of our beautiful daughter, Whitney. He cut the umbilical cord while tears rushed down his face. My aunts and cousins came to see my newborn baby in the hospital and brought gifts. Albert came to pick me up the next day, helped me into the car, and took me home. Again he became the gentleman I knew before he became confused about my pregnancy.

Unfortunately, he went right back to his ways of leaving me behind while he saw other women. He worked at a pizza restaurant very near the apartment complex where I lived. I called him so often that the manager was certain that I was crazy.

Christmas in the year of 2000, when Whitney was just five months old, I called my father on the phone.

"Merry Christmas, Daddy! Whitney and I want to come and see you for Christmas!"

"Don't you bring any black people to my house!" he said as he hung up the phone. I would have done anything so my father would accept me for who I was and agree to meet his granddaughter.

That same year I received a Christmas card from my Grandma Murphree (Dad's mom) wishing me a Merry Christmas, but telling me that she did not approve of my black baby. Again I faced rejection from someone I loved.

My mother drove down to see her first grandbaby. I was shocked that she came at all because she had made it clear that she didn't want me to have any black children. As she entered the house with a cigarette in her hand I said, "Mom, the smoke is not good for the baby. You're going to have to smoke outside!"

"I'll be d***ed if I'm going to stand outside and smoke my cigarette in the hot a** sun!" she said. She was angry because she didn't want to go outside to smoke after a lifetime of smoking inside her house. So she left my house and immediately drove three hours back home, furious at not being able to smoke inside my house.

My mother often called me to complain about my having a black baby and being with a black man. As soon as she would start spitting out racial slurs like "nigger," I would hang up the phone. I told her that if she wanted a relationship with me, she would have to accept my decisions and leave the word "nigger" out of her vocabulary. Eventually she decided that she did want to build our relationship and she learned to accept her first grandbaby even though Whitney was biracial. Our relationship finally flourished. We spoke on the phone nearly every day. And she grew to love Whitney.

Albert's mother flew in from Nigeria to see her granddaughter, her new bundle of joy. It felt so good that his parents accepted our daughter regardless of her skin color. Albert's mother told him that the best thing for him to do was to marry me. However, Albert didn't heed her advice.

When Whitney was five months old, the Immigration Department picked him up at his house and took him to detention in Louisiana. He called me at work and said, "I got arrested by the INS."

"What is INS?" I asked. I had no idea what he meant by INS, my first thought was insurance. "How come they arrested you for your insurance? They usually just give a ticket for that." He explained that INS stood for Immigration Naturalization Service and that he had let his student visa expire. That was my first time hearing about his immigration status, and I began to realize what a serious situation it was. Albert's mother sent money for bail, and he was able to come back home about a month later.

While he was in detention, Albert wrote me letters saying "Crystal, I'm sorry for the way I've treated you! I want to be a part of our baby's life!" Before his plea, I had decided I was going to go on with my life without him and would no longer deal with the way that he had treated me. However, one day after he got out of detention, he called and asked me the question that I had wanted to hear from him for such a long time, "*Will you marry me?*"

I smiled from ear to ear when I heard his words. I could do nothing but say, "Yes, I will marry you!" After all, I did love him and wanted to spend the rest of my life with him.

We drove back to Louisiana together for his immigration court hearing. After the hearing, we went to the nearest courthouse to get married. While crying and laughing at the same time, I said, "I do!" He smiled and said, "I do!" We both agreed to be married "till death do us part."

When my mother heard about our marriage, she told me that it would not last up to twelve years. I felt that she wanted to see my marriage fail, and I wondered why she specified *twelve years*. Was it because her marriage to my father lasted exactly twelve years?

We drove back to my apartment and lived there together. I stayed at home taking care of Whitney and Albert worked construction jobs. Albert's mother came back to America to visit again and she sent us plane tickets to meet at his sister's house in Georgia. There I met my sisters-in-law, Titilayo and Funmilayo, for the first time. Before Albert's mother returned to Nigeria, she advised us to move to Georgia so that her children could be together and look after one another. So we flew back to Arkansas, packed everything into a U-Haul, and drove to Georgia again to move in with his sister until we could find a house of our own.

Not too long after we had moved to Georgia, my sister-in-law's husband called everybody into the living room one day shortly after he returned from work. He had news to deliver. He spoke in Hausa and the only word I understood was "Mommy." Seeing their tears and hearing their screams, I knew in my heart they had just lost their mother.

Albert looked at me in tears and said, "Mommy died."

He went straight to the closet of the bedroom and lay down on the floor and cried his heart out. I tried to open the door and console him, but he refused to let me in. He just wanted to be alone. I cried for them and wished she could have lived longer. My heart ached for my husband.

When we finally got our own place again, I put Albert's mother's picture in a frame. I also hired an artist to paint a portrait of his mother for him for Christmas. I knew how close he was to his mother and how much she meant to him. When you love a man, what hurts him will hurt you.

Albert and I still had our issues. We were lost, living very worldly lives. Living for Christ was something that didn't even enter our thoughts. None of our friends were true Christians.

I had made horrible decisions and my life was a complete mess. I even got arrested for one of my stupid decisions and spent some time in jail. I lived in complete darkness. Now I'm aware that what I was doing was because of the darkness in my life, the same darkness that comes from not living for Jesus. A life lived for Jesus sheds light on all of it and helps us to see the life that we were actually living. He gives us wisdom.

Albert often fell asleep in his recliner with an empty 40-ounce beer bottle in his hand. We had both had adulterous relationships and we had friends who were bad influences on our lives and our daughter's life. We lived like that for several years until that awful day when Albert was stopped for a broken taillight and ended up being arrested by the INS again and being deported.

7

We were both at a loss for words in those few minutes that were changing our lives forever. We knew our family was being torn apart.

As I cried, I had no idea how I was going to cope with being a single mother and living without Albert. I wanted to die right there on the side of the street. I felt like I was the last person on the earth. Cars passed and people craned their necks curiously. The laws of my country were hurting me in a profound way. American Immigration makes it extremely difficult to become legal once you have allowed the visa to expire.

My mind was bombarded with fearful and angry thoughts: *How can they take my husband away from us and then go home to their families and sleep well at night? How will I explain to our little girl that her father is gone? What kind of childhood memory will be put into her mind by seeing her daddy put into a police car and taken away from us? How do I explain to my four-year-old that the police have taken her daddy away?*

So many thoughts and worries rushed through my head. I knew I had to be strong for our daughter even though I felt powerless without my husband. He was my right hand, my support, and my strength.

After the police car drove away with Albert, I dropped Whitney at preschool. As soon as I entered the room, I lost total control of my emotions. I cried to the teacher and told her what had just happened, putting her in an awkward position. She didn't really know what to say to me except that she was sorry. Many Americans don't like the fact that immigrants are in America, but their views might change if they saw how people live in other countries. Or perhaps if they happened to fall in love with someone from another country.

I called my boss at work to tell her what had happened and that I would be a little bit late getting to work. I realized this was definitely no time to be missing work since I had a child to support and bills to pay. I knew it was going to be impossible for me to make all the payments solely from my income because it had taken both of our salaries to pay all of the bills. It was difficult for me to focus, not knowing what the next step in my life would be.

We had moved to Marietta, Georgia, from Fayetteville, Arkansas, and had no family near, except for Albert's sister. I called my sister-in-law to tell her what had happened, and she was distraught that her brother was being sent back to Nigeria. She couldn't believe what had just happened.

She said, "You should bring Whitney to me, so you can go to work and figure out what to do." I wanted to keep Whitney with me, but I also needed to work.

A 60-year-old woman that I worked with needed a place to live, so I agreed to let her move into Whitney's room if she would pay half of the expenses. Albert and I had two cars and two car payments, so I also let her take one of the cars as long as she agreed to make the payments on the car loan. Anybody that came to visit me would ask, "Is that your mother?" It was so difficult to get used to having someone other than my husband occupying space in my house, but that was just how it had to be for the moment.

That was the beginning of my path to finding strength to do what was necessary as I passed through this new chapter in my life. I was confused and had no idea what was going to happen to our family. I knew nothing about the process of filing immigration paperwork for my husband.

A cousin of Albert's from Florida, a Nigerian whom I had never met, learned of Albert's arrest and immediately flew in to check on Whitney and me. He also went to see Albert in the detention center where detainees are held before being deported to their countries. I was touched by his concern for us. None of my family members came over to check on us. It game me insight into the difference between the culture of my American family and the culture of the Nigerian family into which I was married.

Albert had come to America when he was just sixteen years old and had spent ten years in the United States. Faced with going back to Nigeria after all those years brought him mixed emotions: happiness to finally see his father again, but fear of being forced to go back unexpectedly.

Another cousin flew in to see Albert, and he was an immigration lawyer. After he left, he called me many times and I asked him countless questions since I knew nothing of the whole immigration process. His Nigerian accent made it hard for me to understand him; either that or I was just so stressed and confused that I couldn't understand him. Eventually, I called my cousin and told her that I was going to put her on a three-way call so that she could help me ask him questions and see if she could make some sense of what he was saying. He kept telling me that I would have to prove hardship to the Immigration Agency before they would ever give him a visa back into America. I was completely lost.

A few days later, the phone rang and it was Albert. I was so relieved to hear his voice that I burst into tears. I thought I would never see or hear from him again. I cried out my frustration and fear for the future, telling him of the choices we had, according to what his cousin had told me.

If we filed for Albert's visa, they could keep him locked up longer since there was no telling how long the process would take. Finally, we chose to follow the other option of allowing the process of deportation to take place.

I drove with Whitney to see Albert at the detention center. I sat down in the chair in the visitors' room where we could see him behind the glass. Whitney sat in my lap while we visited.

"Why did you bring Whitney here? I said you shouldn't bring her to see me like this." Albert said. But I thought it was important for Whitney to see her daddy no matter what the circumstances were. In my mind, I knew that one day she would know the truth about her father, that he was not a bad person.

I wished I could pinch myself and wake up from this nightmare. I felt so helpless and just wished that my husband could come home with me and that it would all be over. I cried as I looked at him through the glass, "Albert, I truly love you and want us to spend the rest of our lives together!"

Albert spent three months in jail until they sent him back to Nigeria. In the meantime, we wrote to each other and called—that was our relationship for those months.

In Albert's letters he quoted verses from the Bible, which was something that was not normal to hear from him. Jesus and the Bible were just not a part of our lives. Albert told me that he had given his life to Christ. I didn't pay too much attention to what he was telling me about Jesus, although it comforted me. He shared this passage with me:

James 1:2-13 My brothers and sisters, when you have many kinds of trouble, you should be full of joy, because you know that these troubles test your faith, and this will give you patience. Let your patience show itself perfectly in what you do. Then you will be perfect and complete and will have everything you need. But if any of you needs wisdom, you should ask God for it.

Just before Albert's arrest, it seemed like our lives were finally settling down and we were doing well. At least we thought we were doing well, having our lives on the right track. Little did we know that we were lacking the one thing in our lives which prevented us from reaching our fullest potential. We were not Christians and we had never acknowledged or lived our lives for Jesus Christ. We were both lost and living in the world. What we thought was the most important thing at that time, ended up to be the least important. We were working hard to gain material things and thought that was what we needed. We had no idea that the lives we were living and the decisions we were making were detrimental to our future, for us and for our child. We were basically living life with our eyes shut. That is just what sin does: it blinds us from recognizing our blessings and seeing what our lives would be like without sin—this is the devil's mission.

The last time I made a visit to Albert in the detention center before he was flown back to Nigeria, I parked, put my purse inside the trunk and went inside the facility. When I came back out, I opened the trunk to get my purse and it was not there. I remembered putting my purse in the trunk! Clearly, I was not aware of my surroundings and someone must have been watching me. My phone and debit card were inside the purse that was stolen, so I couldn't call anybody, and I couldn't get money from the ATM.

I never suspected that this was a bad area of town, but I was obviously mistaken. Somebody had also attempted to steal my car. The ignition cylinder had been removed in the attempt to start the car and there was no way of driving the car in that condition. I looked up at this tall building in Atlanta that was keeping my husband from me and just wished he could come out of there and help me. I wondered if he could see me from the window while I was standing outside across the street in the blazing sun.

I managed to get help from someone nearby who showed me how to start the car with a screwdriver. I've always wondered if he was the one who tried to steal it since he knew how to remedy the situation. The car was a stick shift and I had to make sure that it didn't stall. I wouldn't be able to restart the car with a screw driver by myself. It was another one of those moments where I had to be strong for myself and for our daughter. All we had was each other.

A few weeks later while I was driving down the road, my car was hit by another car. By this point, I was overwhelmed with all the problems that were coming my way. My body hurt and my mind ached. I wasn't sure I could continue on like that. I didn't understand why all of these things were happening to me.

I wondered, *What did I do to deserve all of this?* All these things gave meaning to the saying I had heard: *When it rains, it pours.*

After the accident I tried calling my mother, even though she lived 11 hours away from us at the time. Two days passed and I still had not heard from her. She wasn't answering my calls. Since she had her home phone calls forwarded to her cell phone, she never missed a call. I could count on reaching her at any time of the day, no matter what. I became worried and called the police station in Bauxite, Arkansas.

"Bauxite Police Station, how may I help you?" the officer said.

"Um, Hello." I stuttered. "I need someone to go and check on my mother. I've been calling her and she hasn't answered her phone in several days!"

"What is the address, please?" the officer asked.

I gave him the address of my mother's house, and then I waited. She lived alone, so nobody would have known if something happened.

A short time later the phone rang. It was the sheriff. He said, "I'm sorry, but we found your mother inside the house and she is dead." I screamed and cried. Once again my world was shattered.

The police officer said, "Do you have anyone there with you? Will you be okay?"

I said, "Yes, my four-year-old daughter is here." That was the truth; she was the only one that I had at that time.

Whitney came to me, hugged me and said, "Mommy, I'm sorry."

I thought, "How could it be that the two people so important in my life had been taken away from me?" I felt so alone and the world seemed so cold.

My mother had died in her recliner. There was a note on the door that said, "I'm sick, come on in." They found a glass of tea on the table next to her and a Reese's chocolate cup on the floor beside her. She had told me she wasn't feeling well the last time I talked to her, but I never imagined she was seriously ill. My mother's body was decomposed since she had died a few days earlier. When I imagined how her body must have looked after being there for several days, the pain became even worse.

My mother had heart disease, had suffered several heart attacks, and had gone through triple bypass surgery a few years earlier. She survived multiple heart attacks, but never made the decision to stop smoking. During one visit to the doctor when I accompanied her, the doctor had asked her, "Have you stopped smoking?" Before she could even answer I said, "No, she hasn't!" She was furious with me because I had told the doctor the truth. She continually told him she had stopped smoking.

After being told about the death of my mother, I had to make the phone call to deliver the news to my older brother. He answered the phone and I said, "Billy, sit down somewhere, I need to tell you something!"

I asked again, "Are you sitting down?"

I'm not sure why I insisted that he sit down, maybe to prevent him from falling after hearing such painful news. As tears ran down my face I said, "The Bauxite police just called and told me that Mom died."

He screamed and cried, "No! No! Please tell me my mother is not dead! I have unfinished business with her!" I could feel his pain of not being able to tell his mother, "Good-bye!" or "Sorry!" or "I love you!" We both wished that we weren't so far apart so that we could console each other while we mourned the death of our mother.

My brother hadn't spoken to our mother in nearly two years, even though he lived just 10 minutes from her. Apparently, his wife and our mother had a disagreement. His wife made my brother choose between her and his mother. Sadly, their marriage didn't last long after the death of our mother. To add to my brother's pain, a few years later, he received the heart-breaking news that his daughter and ex-wife were killed in a car accident.

I found out about the death of my mother while Albert was in transit to Nigeria. As soon as he arrived in Nigeria, he was told about the death of my mother. It was so difficult to bear this loss while Albert and I were separated from each other. Her death was just two years after the loss of his mother in 2003.

I called my Aunt Jean, my mother's sister, and her son answered the phone. As soon as he answered I cried, "Mom died!" while crying uncontrollably.

I was in shock and I desperately needed to receive some sort of comfort after hearing about the death of my dear mother while I was alone in our apartment. My cousin didn't know what to say and he handed the phone to his mother while giving her the news. All I could hear was wailing and crying in the background. Nobody could believe that Rita had passed on at such a young age; she was only fifty years old. Her own mother was still alive to witness the death of her daughter.

As soon as my aunts and their daughters in Fayetteville heard the news, they said that I should come to be with them right away.

I wondered if my mother's death was caused in part by loneliness. At the time of her passing, she was married to a man from Mexico. I wondered how she was able to have a relationship with someone that didn't speak English since she didn't speak Spanish. They did use a translator at times. Mom sometimes attempted to speak Spanish when she called me, and she seemed to be happy for a time. She thought she had found a man to love her and help her take care of the house. She had hired a lawyer to help get her husband's green card. The lawyer advised that her husband should go back to Mexico for nine months while they filed. While he was gone, Mom called his number in Mexico to speak to her husband. She was surprised when a woman answered the phone.

"I'm Ensivio's wife; you need to stop calling here!"

My mother's spirit was broken. She was hurt and lonely. She had been hurt so many times and it took a toll on her. She became paranoid and seemed to be losing her mind. She had gone through so much in her lifetime and she was weak.

Earlier I had called to tell her that I was going to Nigeria soon and I wanted to send a ticket for her to come visit me in Georgia before I left. Her response was to say, "I'm not going there so that I will be killed because Immigration is watching me!"

I said, "Mom, what are you talking about, the people in Immigration don't want to kill you!"

"Then how come I sent a letter to them and the postal truck was blown up!"

She even refused to turn on her TV because she thought someone was going to hear every word she said. She also thought she was taking a risk by being on the phone with me. I didn't know what was happening with my mom. She begged me, "Please come back home!"

I told her, "I can't come back home; I have to go to Nigeria to be with Albert!"

My heart ached for my mom; she wasn't herself anymore. I wanted to go visit her, but so much was happening in my life that I didn't know what to do. Before I could make arrangements to see her, she died.

I packed up everything in our house, rented and loaded a U-Haul truck, and drove 11 hours back to Fayetteville. I never knew I was so tough until the only choice for me was to be strong. I persuaded one of my husband's close friends to ride with me in hopes that he would be able to help me drive part of the way. Surprisingly, he was too afraid to drive such a large truck and I had to drive the whole way alone. As soon as we reached our destination, he got on a Greyhound bus and went back to Georgia.

It was time for my brother and me to handle the estate of our deceased mother, but I was not ready to go to the house where she had died, especially after hearing how the house smelled because of her decomposed body. Nor was I ready to go through the things in her house. It was overwhelming since she was a "pack rat" who kept everything and never threw anything out. Our mother was a compulsive hoarder.

She had kept everything: from the clothes she wore when she married my dad twenty five years earlier, to every letter that was ever written to her, to child support checks from our father, and many things that belonged to her deceased father, to washers, dryers and cars that no longer worked. She kept a record of everything that anybody had ever done to her. It all brought back bad memories from my childhood.

There was a picture of me when I was a just a little girl. I was lying on the couch with my father, and his arm was around me. As I looked at the picture, I wondered what happened and why I was no longer his little girl. I asked myself, *How come I don't have any memories with my father?* As I found more pictures of me with my mother, I burst into tears and fell to the ground. I couldn't comprehend the fact that she was gone so soon—just as we were beginning to have a fragile, yet growing relationship.

I went through as many papers as I could in case there was anything of importance. At some point, I could no longer dig through those papers because I was afraid of what state of mind I might be in after looking through all of these things. It was incredibly painful when I found a letter that seemed like a will. One of her requests was that she could donate her eye to Dennis, the man who had molested me and was missing an eye. I also found the newspaper article about me being abused at the age of 13. My mother had held onto that clipping for all of those years.

Billy and I took any pictures or papers of importance or sentimental value, and then called an auctioneer to sell the rest of her things.

I decided to drive her car back to where I was staying with my cousin, so that we could sell it. The driver side window had a problem and it wouldn't roll down, and the windshield wipers didn't work. It started raining very hard while I was driving, I could barely see where I was going.

When I arrived back at my cousin's I sat in her backyard and burned every single paper. I no longer cared if I was burning anything of importance. My mom never forgot about the past but held on to it as if it was a prize. Her attitude and actions were rather unfortunate. I, on the other hand, wanted to forget about my past and move on, not allowing my past to affect my future. But sometimes it's just not that simple. I never saw many pictures of my father and mother together, only her with us children. At that point, I had so many questions, but it was too late to ask her. I couldn't understand why my mother did some of the things that she did.

Aunt Jean and I chose the casket and made all of the other necessary arrangements. We were advised by the undertaker not to have an open casket because of her decomposed body. We followed his advice to prevent having that as our last impression of our mother.

On September 4, 2005, my birthday, I visited my mother's body in the funeral home. My brother, who was closer to our father than me, asked our father if he would come to our mother's funeral because my brother felt like he needed the support. When our father showed up at the funeral, it was the first time I had seen him in five years—since I was pregnant with Whitney. There he saw my daughter for the first time.

Only a handful of people showed up to pay their respects to our mother. Aunt Jean looked at Dad and said, "Crystal is going to Africa soon."

"Are you going to eat some monkey soup?" he sneered. My aunt and I kept quiet, trying not to be offended by his words. He then asked when I was leaving and I answered that it would be in a few weeks.

We learned that Mom had a safe deposit box at her bank, so my cousin and I drove three hours to the bank to see what was inside the box. We thought we might find a will or documentation for her land. I was almost certain that we would not find a large sum of money because of the way that my mother lived before she died.

Once we reached the bank, we discovered that the key did not fit, so we had to pay a locksmith 70 dollars to open the box. We found that there was absolutely nothing inside. Eight years later, my brother has still had a hard time forgiving me for opening that safe deposit box without him. He was convinced there had been money inside and that I had kept it all to myself. I will never understand how Billy thought she had any money, especially the way she struggled to survive in the last years of her life. In fact, she worried about finances all her life.

A few years later while searching on Facebook, I found some old classmates and friends that had lived near our house when we were children. Several of them told me they were very happy to see that I was alive. Apparently, my brother had told them I had killed myself in front of him after the death of our mother.

If I had known that opening that box without him would cost me our relationship, I would gladly have allowed Billy to be the one to pay 70 dollars to the locksmith and drive three hours to find nothing. This was a lesson learned: people are far more important than money.

Staying with my extended family after the funeral did not go well. It made me regret ever deciding to leave my apartment in Marietta. If I had it to do over again, I would not have moved, but would have just stayed put.

Whitney and I stayed with a cousin until she asked us to leave, just two weeks after the death of my mother. I was hurt, but packed up everything to go live with another cousin for a short time while I waited for Albert to send airline tickets for us to travel to Nigeria. Soon I was told indirectly to get out of that home. It was hard moving my daughter around from place to place while I dealt with death of my mother and the absence of my husband.

In desperation I called Albert, "I don't have anywhere to stay now! How will I be able to come to Nigeria?" We didn't have enough money for Whitney and me to fly to Nigeria at the time.

"Let me talk to Daddy and I will call you back." he said. Thankfully, in a few weeks Albert called to say, "My father gave me the money for your tickets!" I was so relieved. At last Whitney and I would have a place to call home again. I spent the last few weeks in America with my Aunt Jean.

I have forgiven these people in my heart. In addition, they have also been able to forgive me for some unwise decisions that I have made in the past. I am not telling of these things to hurt anyone. These events were just a part of my journey.

8

Many Americans dislike being put out of their comfort zones. I have heard it said that America has a "me" culture; and having grown up in America, I had the same "me" traits before I went to Nigeria. The upcoming experience would eventually make me into a more grateful and considerate person.

Before I arrived in Nigeria, Albert made me as fully aware of what I would be facing while living there. He did not want to make life seem any better than it really was. At the time, I didn't care what the conditions or circumstances would be, as long as we could be together as a family. And at the time, moving to Nigeria was our only option since Albert was barred from re-entering America for ten years. A close cousin told me that she would give me three months until I would come right back to America.

Later I understood that I could have filed for Albert's green card since I am an American citizen and we are married, but we had to prove extreme hardship since he was deported. According to the U. S. Citizenship and Immigration Services (USCIS), hardship cannot be for minor reasons. Extreme hardship is vaguely defined as greater than the normal hardship the qualifying relative can be expected to experience if the alien is denied admission. We didn't have any real hardships according to Immigration, regardless of all the actual hardships we were facing. With that in mind, I thought it would be impossible to get a visa for my husband. The separation of family is not seen as a hardship in the Immigration system.

It was a matter of making a choice: staying in America and finishing my education, which I had just started, or joining my husband in Nigeria. Some people told me it would be best for me to stay in America and finish my education, but I reasoned that it would be better for me to go to Nigeria, so that we could be together as family. It meant more to me for my daughter to grow up with her father.

Besides that, I wanted to be with my husband forever. He was all I had.

While I put my education on hold, I visualized the house where we would live. I imagined us not having much, but at least we would be together. Albert told me that there was no electricity and no running water. "Where will we get water?" I asked.

"Someone will fetch the water from a well. There will be no problem finding someone that can hand-wash the clothes and get the water for us," he said.

I was flabbergasted by the fact that all of our clothes would be washed by hand and even more astonished that someone would wash them for us. I asked, "Who would possibly want to hand wash all of our clothes?"

He replied, "Don't worry; we can pay someone to do that. You can live life like a princess!"

I was incredulous to learn that there were people living in this world without electricity and running water. I didn't understand why. I never once thought about how we got electricity in America or if people in other parts of the world had it. The only time the electricity went off in America was when we had a storm or if you didn't pay your bill on time. Even when the power went off, everybody would eagerly light candles throughout the house, always making the moment memorable.

My main concern was about what I would eat, so I asked Albert "Are their eggs, chicken, bread, and potatoes?"

He replied, "Of course, we have all that in Nigeria, there is even a Church's Chicken in Lagos!" (I later found out that Lagos was eleven hours away from where we would reside).

He assured me that there was a four-bedroom house that his father was giving us to live in and they were doing some renovations before I arrived. I was excited about the thought of reuniting with my husband and even more thrilled that we were getting a house given to us. They all knew that Americans had a different lifestyle, and they did their best to make sure the house was comfortable for me. That brought me great joy.

Finally, I had our plane tickets to go to Nigeria to rejoin my husband. I had missed him so much, and Whitney would be able to reunite with her father after nine long months of separation. I was so grateful to my father-in-law who paid for our tickets. If he had not done so, our separation would have been much longer. I rented a car to drive eleven hours back to Georgia where we would get our flight because Arkansas didn't have an international airport.

The day before our flight, my sister-in-law asked me, "Where do you want to eat before you leave?"

"I want to eat at Golden Corral!" I said. That was our last American meal. It felt like she was asking someone on death row what they would like to eat before they died.

We had an eleven-hour layover in London. I had four suitcases, four carry-ons, and a four-year-old daughter who was too young to carry anything. There was a cart to use for carrying the suitcases, but unfortunately all of them would not fit on just one cart. So I was left to push two carts and watch after my young daughter. I finally used a shoestring to tie both carts together and pulled it like a train with Whitney on the top.

We went to look for something to eat inside the airport. "Yes, how can I help you?" a man asked in his British accent.

"I'll have some French fries and a soda," I said.

"We have chips, is that what you want?"

"Ok, that's fine!"

He came to the table a short time later with soda water and French fries. I thought, *How come he told me they only have chips, but he brought French fries; and why did he give me soda water!* I later figured out that next time I should say "chips" and a "Coke." Some Americans call Coke "soda." I told the waitress that I wanted a Coke, since there was no way I could drink soda water. Americans call chips, "French fries", while "chips" are thinly sliced and fried potatoes sold in bags.

Jet lag set in. I was exhausted from the long flight and I had to find my way to the other airport in London to catch my next flight. Luckily, I found a family that offered to help me find my way and helped with my luggage. I attempted to call Albert from a pay phone, but couldn't figure out how to make the call. One of the flight attendants came looking for me since I was the last one to get on the plane. I was sluggish from being in a far different time zone, I was traveling across the world for the first time in my life, I was responsible for my daughter, and I was doing it all alone.

When we arrived in Nigeria, the pilot said, "We are arriving in Abuja, Nigeria, and we hope that you enjoyed your flight. It is 32 degrees outside." I was surprised to hear that it could be so cold in Nigeria. I looked at Whitney saying, "Oh my goodness, it's cold outside. Hurry and put your jacket on before we get off the plane!"

Once I stepped out of the plane I felt scorching heat. I didn't know

Peace in an Unlikely Place   —   Crystal Owonubi

that the pilot meant 32 degrees Celsius, rather than Fahrenheit, as I was used to hearing in America. The airport was terribly hot because there was no electricity and no air conditioning.

I followed the rest of the Nigerians that had gotten off the plane. While observing my surroundings, I noticed the men speaking a foreign language and wearing what looked like dresses. It was actually the common cultural clothing. I was nervous and didn't know what to expect from the Immigration officials and others in the airport while entering this country. The Immigration officer looked at my passport, looked back up at me and said, "Are you married to a Nigerian?"

"Yes, Sir!" I said, in hopes that I would not be rejected for my pale skin. After all, I was used to discrimination against one's color, coming from America. He must have noticed that my last name was Owonubi from the Yoruba tribe, so he stamped my passport, smiled and said, "Our wife, you are welcome to Nigeria!"

I smiled and said, "Thank You" and then I passed through the gate to look for my luggage. Some boys helped me get my entire assortment of luggage, loaded it onto the carrier and pushed it outside for me. I thought, *Wow, how come they didn't have this kind of service at the airport in London?*

Some Nigerians in America had told me to be careful because corrupt officials might try to take my things away from me at the airport. But they didn't even bother to check my luggage as I left the terminal.

I was the last person to get through Immigration and Customs. Albert was anxiously waiting; we hadn't spoken to each other since I left America the day before.

It was a special moment to see Whitney and her father reunite. Watching Whitney run to her father saying, "Daddy!" reminded me of a scene in a movie. I held back tears of mixed emotions: joy, pain, and a feeling of relief that the journey was over and that we were finally together again.

I didn't realize then that I was embarking upon another journey, one of adapting to a new culture that was different from anything I had ever experienced; this journey that my Lord Jesus Christ was taking me through. I looked at Albert and we hugged each other. Then he introduced me to his brothers as they welcomed me to Nigeria.

I had no problem with the Nigerians in the airport; they welcomed me with open arms because I was a foreigner who married a

Nigerian. Any foreign woman who marries into their culture is called "our wife." Even if the woman is not foreign, she can be known as "our wife," because she has entered into the husband's family. This is basically their way of saying, "You have married into our culture and family, and we accept you with open arms." They are very grateful and happy for women who have married Nigerians and have moved there; after all, they know that we could live easier lives in America. And they appreciate those who choose to live in their country. This was the opposite of what I was used to, growing up rejected by people and family because of my Nigerian husband. I felt loved and honored by these people.

Leaving the airport, I noticed that even the air was different from the air in America. What looked like fog to me in the early evening was a thin cloud of dust. As we got into the vehicle, I noticed that the car was also dusty. I felt like I had entered into a desert.

The first night in Abuja we stayed at my brother-in-law's house. I was hot and tired and just wanted to take a bath and go to sleep. Someone warmed my bath water, put it in a bucket and set it in the bathtub. I had no idea where the hot water came from, but I knew it didn't come from the faucet. I cooled it with some tap water and soaped up. It was difficult trying to figure out how to wash my hair with a bucket of water and a bowl. From inside the bathroom I called out, "Albert!" He stepped inside the bathroom and I looked up at him with a head full of suds. "How do I rinse my hair?"

He laughed. "Let me help you!"

You would think common sense would tell me how to rinse my hair, but having grown up with hot water coming out of the faucet and never having to take a bath with a bucket and a bowl, it was a strange experience for me. Eventually, I figured it out and no longer needed my husband's help. It was never easy and I hated carrying a bucket of water to the bathroom to bathe every day. I quickly became irritated and tired of having to warm my bath water with either an electric boiling ring that is placed inside a bucket, or in a pot on the stove.

As I lay down for a short nap under the fan, I felt blessed relief from the excessive heat in Abuja. Suddenly the fan went off and I became extremely hot. I woke up and stepped out of the room and looked at Albert. "Why did you turn off the fan?"

"Welcome to Nigeria!" He laughed.

That was my first time to experience the power going off and they

assured me that it would come back on later. I looked at them with confusion wondering, *How can they bring power, then turn it off and then bring it back again?* I asked, "Why does it have to be like that?"
It was explained to me that there was not enough power generated for the entire country, and they turn it off when necessary.
"And who is 'they'?" I asked.
Albert said, "The power company is called PHCN which stands for Power Holding Company of Nigeria."
The name sure fit the company because they always "held" the power. There was no certain time to expect the power to come on; it simply went on and off unexpectedly. Sometimes the current was so low that it was the same as having no electricity. Sometimes the current was so high that every appliance in the house would blow. Fortunately, somebody could repair the damage for a small fee.
The first meal I had in Nigeria was Quaker Oats. I thought, *Okay, this is not bad. We eat oats in America.* I was happy that it was something that I had eaten before and it looked familiar.
At lunchtime I was given chicken and rice with carrots and green beans. The vegetables were fresh and not soft, like the canned ones in America. I was happy to see chicken since everybody knows what chicken tastes like. I took a bite, kept chewing but couldn't swallow it because the meat was so tough. I had a huge piece of meat in my mouth that would have choked me if I tried to swallow it, so I tried to inconspicuously spit it out. I soon learned that much of the chicken in Nigeria is very tough. There are broilers and then there are local chickens. Broilers are more like the chicken in America. I have always preferred the white meat, which is a typical American food made into chicken strips and nuggets. I was happy that I had not been given the head or the feet of the chicken, which a lot of Nigerians love to eat. I have never heard of Americans eating those! In fact, many of us never even see that part of the chicken unless we live on a farm or work in a chicken factory.
The rice was also different for me. I had never wanted to eat rice in America since there were other options that I preferred, like hamburgers, tacos or pizza. The only time we ate rice growing up was when our mother would cook it for breakfast and add butter and sugar. Little did I know that I would be eating rice almost every day for dinner in the years to come.

The next day it was time to make the three-hour trip to Jos where we would live. There I would meet my father-in-law for the first time and see the house that would become my home. The whole way there I was wide-eyed, viewing the small huts and people carrying firewood or buckets of water on their heads. I asked many questions along the way and admired seeing such a beautiful country. I had never seen anything like it before and I felt honored to have a chance to see the most populous black nation in the world.

Between Abuja, the capital of Nigeria and Jos are many villages consisting of various types of huts. This doesn't mean that there are no standard houses in Nigeria, as some people think about Africa. Most of us only know what we see on TV. A person cannot know what it is like in Nigeria until they have personally been there. Each country in Africa is different, just as each state in Nigeria is different. When I speak of Nigeria, I am speaking from what I know about life in Jos. I was excited to be in a different country!

We traveled on the bumpy road with its many potholes. In a way, it made me think of a movie predicting what it will be like when God comes and the earth splits! The driver had to bob and weave to dodge the "gallops," which could send the car off the road. The driver also had to watch out for other cars that were trying to dodge the potholes on their side of the road and often came into our lane. I was afraid we would have an accident because cars were speeding to get where they were going and passing the slow cars. There were no restrictions on speed limit or on passing cars. I still do not enjoy traveling on those highways because I usually get a major headache from the excessive heat and the swerving; and even my body would ache afterwards. Everybody knows it is dangerous to be on the roads in Nigeria; that is why so many pray before they travel and thank God each time they return safely.

A car came from the other direction flashing its lights at us. "Does that mean there is a cop up ahead?" I said.

Albert assured me, "No, there are not going to be any police cars waiting on the side of the street to catch those that are speeding!" I thought it would be like in America: the police hide to catch oncoming speeders, and cars coming past them warn others by flashing their lights.

We did get stopped at a few checkpoints on the way, operated by men in military uniforms holding guns. This is a normal procedure to protect travelers from armed robbers; but all I could think of was the movie "Hotel Rwanda" and wondered why they were holding guns!

Unfortunately, many times the officials extort the travelers by asking, "Anything for me?" or bringing false charges in an attempt to get paid. The officials at these checkpoints often thought that Albert was my driver instead of my husband; and they thought that I was a missionary because I was white. Sometimes I would put my hand on his head to see how people would react. We were always amused at the expressions of people wondering why I would be touching my driver.

The heat was overwhelming in the car since there was no air conditioning. This was one of the only times in my life that I had been forced to sit in the heat. Albert assured me that the weather would change drastically when we got to the plateau where Jos is located. I was blessed that my husband's family lived in Jos, where the weather is mostly enjoyable throughout the year. I wonder if I would have been able to cope with the heat living anywhere else in Nigeria, where the weather is extremely hot all year.

I was hungry and wished we could stop at a gas station or McDonald's along the way to get some food, but that couldn't happen. What we did see was yam and sweet potatoes being sold by farmers on the roadside. We also saw many vendors carrying healthy snacks such as bananas and "groundnuts" (peanuts) in large trays on their heads near the petrol stations. Petrol (or gasoline) stations in Nigeria are strictly for the sale of fuel, unlike in America where cold drinks or snacks are available. On the road from Abuja to Jos there are definitely no Hershey chocolate bars, Cheetos, or any of the popular snack items found in America.

It is common to have long queues to get fuel for the car. Unlike in America where one pulls up and pumps the fuel without waiting, in Nigeria someone stands at the pump collecting money and pumping the fuel into the cars and motorbikes. The motorbikes are known as "okada" or "achaba." Sometimes after the customer has waited in line for several hours, the station will run out of fuel, or they just decide to stop selling. During my time in Nigeria, I hardly ever went to the gas station myself because of this frustrating process.

We did not find a clean bathroom with toilet paper on our trip to Jos. In fact it is rare to find a public toilet with a seat and running water anywhere. Toilets are usually not clean because of the lack of running water. One has to squat on the roadside and I didn't want to do that. However, at some time or another one may be forced to use that method. Most women carry their own toilet paper in their purse. Some Nigerians do not have toilets in their homes, while others live in some of the nicest homes with fancy bathrooms. The first time I saw someone squatting on the side of the street, I was devastated. I asked a rather stupid question while my eyes bugged open: "What is he doing?"

"He's pooping." Albert answered. It was quite obvious that this man was using the street as a toilet.

"No way, you're not serious! He's just pooping in public like that?" After an exhausting three-hour drive, we arrived at Apata Street in Jos, an area that is densely populated. The house was the biggest one on the entire street, and everyone seemed to be familiar with the so-called "family house." We came to the home where my husband had grown up and I was about to meet my father-in-law. When we pulled up to the gate, the driver honked, and a guard opened the gate. My father-in-law walked out of the house, as if he had been eagerly expecting us. I was nervous to meet my husband's father for the first time, not knowing exactly what to say. I felt so grateful for what he had already done for me by buying our airline tickets before he even met me or knew me. I was graciously accepted by my father-in-law, regardless of my color or culture. I learned that it was okay for me to call him "Daddy." It was quite different from my own father's prejudice against my black husband. It had been a long time since I felt accepted, loved, and appreciated by anyone other than Albert. That day many people came around to greet me and to this day I cannot remember who all came. There were so many people and everything was new to me. Every member in Albert's family came to greet me and made me feel very honored. I could see the joy in Albert's eyes for me to meet his family. I always knew when Albert was happy because his top lip shook while he tried to hide his emotions. When I met my father-in-law's brother, I shook his hand, which is a normal gesture in America. Albert wanted me to bow down to him, which is a respectful gesture in Nigeria. When Albert told me to do that, I looked at him in shock and froze, not having ever done such a thing.

"Why are you telling your wife to bow down when you know that is not her culture?" Albert's father said. He didn't expect me to bow because he knew I was not used to that custom.

For the first week we stayed in my father-in-law's house. The people in there wanted to do everything for me. I could have sat down and told them exactly what I wanted and they would have done it for me since I was a guest in the house. However, I wanted to do things for

Peace in an Unlikely Place — Crystal Owonubi

myself though since I felt they would not know how I wanted it done. After all, we are used to doing everything for ourselves in America.

The next morning I woke up and wanted to take a bath. I was still a bit confused about where to get hot water for bathing. Albert told me that they would heat water outside on the fire for me since there was no electricity. I couldn't refuse the help since I did not know how to start a fire; I had always turned on the tap to get hot water. I had never even cooked outside the house. I learned that it was a luxury to wash dishes or take a bath with hot water flowing out of the faucet at the turn of a wrist.

"I want to blow-dry my hair," I told Albert.

He laughed again, "There is still no electricity! And besides, we will have to get a step-down for the blow-dryer that you brought!"

"Why? What is a step-down?"

"The outlets here are different than the ones in America, so we need a step-down transformer to convert the electricity." he said. I tried hard not to be too irritated.

Breakfast time came and the bread tasted very different from Wonder Bread, a common brand that I often ate in America. Whitney chose to eat the local brand of Nasco Corn Flakes, which were not like the Kellogg's we were accustomed to eating. The nanny, Talatu, brought warm milk to pour over the cereal and then started whipping it as if it was Cream of Wheat or oatmeal. The milk she used was powdered. The only time I had ever used powdered milk was when I ran out of milk at our apartment in America while making Jiffy cornbread. I had asked my neighbor for milk and she gave me powdered milk. Since I had always used fresh milk, I was disgusted at the thought of using powdered milk. Now I found that most Nigerians used powdered milk all the time because of the lack of electricity to run their refrigerators to keep milk cool and because liquid milk is more expensive.

I knew that my daughter was experiencing culture shock when tears ran down her face. "I'm not hungry" she said.

"What's wrong?" I asked.

She wouldn't tell me with Auntie Talatu standing right there, but I guessed what the problem was. Without asking her again, I just looked at Auntie Talatu and explained to her that we eat our cereal with cold milk and wouldn't normally eat it hot because we do not want it to be soggy; we want it to be crunchy. I am not sure that she understood what I was saying, since no one else understood my accent.

I was told that I spoke very fast, but that is normal for anyone when they are speaking their primary language. I had to learn to speak slower if I wanted to be understood. Even my father-in-law could not fully understand me. He once looked at Albert and said, "Laolu, what did your wife say?" (Olaolu is my husband's tribal name, which in Yoruba means "The glory of God has come and it will not end.") Albert explained what I had said that particular time.

The second week in Nigeria was like a nightmare when Whitney started vomiting, having diarrhea and running a fever. Neither one of us knew what was wrong with her. Albert and I told his father who then directed us to the nearby hospital. Albert's father was a doctor himself, but he had retired from his practice. He wrote a short note and signed his name, so that the doctor we wanted to see would accept us right away. I felt special because in America it's not that easy to see a doctor.

We had to put a diaper on our five-year-old because of her uncontrollable bowels. People outside the hospital saw her and immediately told us, "It's malaria!" It was obvious that this was a common disease in Nigeria and the people were used to the symptoms and knew how to treat it. The doctor prescribed medication to treat the malaria, but Whitney could not keep the medication or food in her stomach; anything that went in came right out. She was becoming weaker by the day. I literally thought she was going to die. I was hysterical. The doctor said, "I'm going to put her on a drip (IV) since she can't keep her medication down." That meant she would have to be admitted to the hospital.

Whitney stayed in the hospital for two nights until she gained her strength back and the symptoms subsided. The hospital room did not have an extra place for someone to sleep in order to stay with the patient. I had to share the bed with Whitney. It felt like sleeping on a stone because the mattress was so hard. The nurses were not as compassionate as what I was used to growing up in America. The nurse didn't smile one time. The hospital was also not as nice and comfortable as the hospitals I was used to in America. The toilet smelled awful, the walls needed painting and were dirty and there was no place to get food. Luckily, the hospital was just behind my father-in-law's house, so I could walk there to eat. I brought back an orange Fanta and some chips (French fries) for Whitney and immediately after drinking the Fanta she vomited again. "Doesn't the Coke Company clean these bottles?" I asked. I was so upset that

I thought maybe that was another reason why she was sick.

"Of course! They have to sterilize them!" The doctor replied. The bottles are similar to the classic Coke bottles that used to be common in America. The bottles are sent back to the company and reused.

During that same time, I became sick after drinking "Pure Water." Pure Water is a small, clear bag in the shape of a square filled with water that comes from a borehole, a drilled well. I went back to examine the bag, questioning, "Where does this water come from?" There was no answer, and I was frustrated that Albert's cousins in the house had given me that water to drink.

Looking out the window of Whitney's hospital room, I saw what looked like an oversized lizard, something I had never seen before. I jumped and asked, "What in the world is that thing?"

Albert laughed and said, "It's just a lizard, they are everywhere and they don't bother people!" That was a big relief since it looked scary and I thought it would chase me.

After the experience in the hospital, we learned how to recognize the symptoms of malaria early and treat it before it made one of us sick enough to end up in bed for days. It was useless to go to the doctor and tell him we were running a fever or feeling weak. He would just give us malaria medicine and send us on our way, since the majority of people experiencing the same symptoms most likely have malaria. We learned that we didn't have to spend money and time at the doctor's office when we could easily buy the treatment at a kiosk right outside our house.

It was convenient to be able to buy any type of medicine that we needed without getting a prescription. For the few medications requiring a prescription, we could just call a doctor we knew.

Many days had passed and I was curious about where the house was that we would live in and when would we go there. So Albert took me to see the house. As we were driving down a short dirt lane off of the main road, I had a bad feeling when I saw the run down area on the left side of the road. When he suddenly pulled up to an actual gate on the right side and honked, I felt much better about where I would be living. The house had its own gate unlike the slums next door. Someone opened the gate and we drove into the compound of the four-bedroom house; this was bigger than the two-bedroom apartment we had moved from in America. I went inside the house and felt quite comfortable. I was ready to get our house in order so that we could start living like a family again.

The house was surrounded by a wall which had broken glass bottles embedded on the top to prevent anyone from climbing over. The house also had bars on the doors and windows. My husband and my father-in-law had worked to make sure that the walls were freshly painted, new carpet and tiles were installed; and they bought a new fridge, a stove, and a set of furniture for the living room (parlor) before I arrived.

I had arrived in Nigeria with only 200 dollars to my name, and I wondered how I would survive. I had once read an article about some missionaries who were raising support money to help orphans in Nigeria. It stated, "Missionaries must pay their own expenses, which total about 60,000 dollars for the family to move and set up housekeeping and another 6,000 dollars a month for their general expenses. So far, donations totaling about half of the one-time amount and 4,200 dollars a month toward living expenses have been pledged." Our money situation seemed insignificant compared to the needs of the missionaries.

The suitcases I brought with me contained nothing but clothes, Albert's Xbox and a portable DVD player. The DVD player became our TV until my brother-in-law brought us an extra TV that he had in his house in Abuja. Since there was no bed in the house, Albert took one of the beds from his father's house for us to sleep in.

There were plenty of pots and pans and dishes at the family house, so we were able to go there to get anything we needed. My Aunt Jean had given me a new set of bed sheets before I left for Nigeria, so we used those for a curtain until we could buy a proper one. We took the dining room table that my husband used when he was a child and we refinished it. Eventually we were able to pay a carpenter to make chairs for us. The house was neat and clean and quite acceptable.

The wall surrounding our house was a different matter. A creek on the other side of the wall is a place where many people go to "ease themselves." It was quite common to see men peeing anywhere, at any time. During the dry season, the area became full of feces and urine. When the rains came six months later, a disgusting smell wafted through our back windows.

On the other side of our property was a "beer parlor." I always wished I had the power to make the owner shut it down or use the space for something that would add value to the neighborhood. Every night the beer parlor was filled with drunken men that would come and pee on the wall of our compound. By the next day, cigarette butts, empty liquor bottles, and even dirty condoms littered the area. The beer parlor didn't have proper sewage disposal; instead they had a hole in the wall of the building where they poured everything out. Rotting smells often filled the air.

One time while I was in the kitchen preparing breakfast, a lady came to the door. I wondered what could have brought her to my house so early.

"They found a newborn baby in the creek next to the house!" she said.

"What? Why?" I shouted.

"Somebody delivered their baby and dropped it there!"

"Oh my goodness! Is the baby alive? I want to take the baby!"

"No, the baby is dead!"

I ran outside my house to see a crowd of people looking down from the bridge into the creek. When I got there, I saw the newborn baby which was still covered in amniotic fluid and with the umbilical cord still attached. I stood and stared as many thoughts rushed through my head. A nearby police officer buried the baby in the creek. The new and shocking things I was experiencing in Nigeria seemed to be never-ending.

The children in the neighborhood played outside the wall of our house since that was the only space available. Every bit of space is full because of the huge population. The children of the neighborhood slums would often hang around our gate watching us because we lived in the biggest compound in that area. It probably was like seeing a mansion for them considering they were coming from the one room they shared with their entire family.

Since I couldn't bring any of my things from our home in America because of the excessive cost of shipping them, I had put all of our belongings in storage. We had bought new furniture as well as a new washer, dryer, and deep freezer for our apartment just before we had to leave. We paid for the storage for about a year until we realized that the payments were becoming more than the things were worth. We were not sure how long we would be able to pay for the storage or how wise it was to spend money that way.

Finally, I called my brother and asked him to go to the storage unit and get whatever he wanted inside. I told him only to give us our pictures of Whitney from her birth and the pictures of my mother that I had collected after her death. My trust in him was misplaced because we never saw those pictures again.

Eventually I learned to allow God to console me through his Word when He said that we should not store up things on this earth where moth and rust will eat it; rather store up treasures in Heaven. I realized I was not going to go to Heaven with those pictures and I learned to be grateful that I had my children with me, alive and in good health. My children's lives would not suffer a detrimental effect as a result of not having those pictures; rather, the choices I made from here on out would have more of an effect in their lives.

On the day we moved to our house, I unpacked the clothes and Albert went out to buy some things we needed, like buckets, dustpan, mop, broom, and silverware. When he left the house, he told me, "If you needed anything just ask the children outside the gate to buy it or ask the house-help."

I decided that I wanted to get some lettuce, so I called one of the children outside and asked her, "Please, can you help me buy lettuce?"

The little girl came back with some small plastic bags. I later learned that the bags were called "ledas" (leather bags). The Nigerians in Jos don't pronounce the "r," and the "th" sound is replaced with a "d" or "t" sound. So the girl thought I was asking for "ledas" – leather bags! I sent her to return the bags and tried to pronounce lettuce very clearly to her. This time she came back with cabbage! Obviously, speaking clearly to her did not help her understand me better. I gave up.

I looked at her and said, "Thank you."

If I continued to speak like an American, they wouldn't know what I was saying. Eventually, I learned to speak more like the Nigerians in order to be understood. I ended up sounding so much like them that some people said I sound just like a Jos girl.

There were many children in the front of the house who came to see the white woman that moved into the area. They stared at me and said, "You are beautiful!"

One day there were lots of people with about fifty buckets lined up in the front of the house. They wanted to fetch water from our tap. I had no idea what to do or what to say to these people. I didn't know if they were supposed to be there or not. The man working for my husband didn't see a problem with it, so I kept quiet, even though I didn't like it at all. I felt as if my privacy was being invaded. As soon as I told Albert that it bothered me, he let the house-help know not to allow people inside the compound. The tap water only came about once a month, or whenever the Water Board decided to turn it on in our area. Eventually the water stopped coming inside our house completely because the neighbors broke the pipes near their house so they could get the water. During the times when there was no water flowing in the pipes, the neighbors would knock at our gate asking if they could fetch water from our well. I couldn't refuse them; after all, water is life. But if it was dry season when they came, I would be a bit on edge worrying that the well would dry up. They took so much water that the remaining water would be brown. That meant the water level was severely low.

People called our house-help "Black." His name was Christopher, but since he was so dark skinned, somebody had given him that nickname. He helped around the house; hand-washed our clothes, fetched water from the well to store in large containers, cleared the compound grass with a hoe in the rainy season, and went to buy anything I needed. There were small shops near our house where he could buy things for us. He was a very hard working man, yet he could not read or write. We paid him monthly, allowed him to eat our food and tried to encourage him to save his money. However, he never saved a dime. The 5,000 naira (about 30 dollars US) he received each month was more than he had ever had in his entire life. His eyes would light up when we paid him. He said he was going to take a picture of the packs of spaghetti and Indomie (Ramen Noodles) inside my kitchen to show his family in the village. I was surprised that someone wanted to take a picture of the food in my kitchen.

That was the beginning of my understanding of how there are many people in Nigeria who lack food.

The average American grows up with a fridge full of food, while the Nigerians I knew only had leftover food, meat, or drinks (water) in the fridge; and that is only if they were privileged enough to own a refrigerator. Even if people have the money to fill the fridge with food, the lack of power makes it impossible to keep the food fresh, unless they have inverters installed in their house to provide auxiliary power like the richer Nigerians, the missionaries or the government officials have. The majority of the time our fridge was empty with only water inside due to the lack of electricity.

Depending on the family, some Nigerians eat very little meat and some cannot afford to buy drinking water. They are forced to drink the impure well water or whatever water they find. There is a great disparity in the standard of living between the rich and the poor in Nigeria.

Black diligently hand-washed all of our clothes for us. One day I noticed that all of my clothes were getting bigger. One side would be longer than the other, and the necks of my shirts were drooping. I realized he was putting all of his strength into washing my clothes using his big strong hands. I had to ask him to be gentler when washing the clothes since they were not stained and didn't need to be scrubbed so hard.

Getting clothes in Nigeria is not as easy as it is in America. The only options are second-hand items that are donated from developed countries or brand new imported clothes, which are grossly overpriced. By the time they are hand-washed and dried in the African sun a few times, even the expensive items look much like the second-hand clothes. The clothes in the market that come from China tend to fall apart after one washing. Some people call them "China for Nigeria." The second-hand clothes were of better quality than the ones from China so I chose to buy second-hand for my family. Occasionally we got clothes from America if we could get someone to mail it to us.

After the laundry discussion with Black, I willingly agreed to try out this whole hand-washing thing, but I looked like a rookie while trying to rub the cloth together. Black just laughed at me. I had the most difficult time and wondered how I would ever be able to wash all the clothes in the house by hand if I ever had to do all of it by myself. The washing detergent often left painful rashes on my hands. Surprisingly, after awhile I became proficient at hand-washing clothes and my hands became accustomed to the harsh detergent. I actually had times when I enjoyed sitting outside washing our clothing.

Cleaning has always been an enjoyable task for me, but I needed help fetching water from the well because my body was not strong enough to work that hard. Many Nigerians have been carrying water since childhood and they do it without much thought. I watched people fill the buckets full of water, pick them up, and place them on their heads. I thought I was too weak to do that. However, after living in Nigeria for a while, I just had to try it. Amazingly, I had no problem at all lifting the bucket to my head! It was a little painful sitting up there though, but that made me realize how sturdy Nigerian people are. They are very strong individuals because of the conditions they have to endure every day. Yet they still smile and carry on cheerfully because of their faith in God.

I also tried fetching water from a well to see what it was like; it gave me a mental picture of what life was like for our ancestors in America before that land developed. It takes a lot of work to fill containers with water from the well every day for the entire house. I was fortunate to have someone to do that part for me. A lot of valuable time is spent hand-washing clothes and getting water, time that could be spent doing other productive work.

Black slept in our "Boys Quarters" (small outbuildings behind the house used for staff housing, guests or rental property). He began hanging out with youth in the neighborhood and he also started drinking. One day I looked out my back window and noticed he had a friend inside the room with him. I walked out my back door and down the steps. As I stood in front of his door, I noticed a strong smell of marijuana. He had placed a towel at the bottom of the door to prevent the smell from seeping out, but it didn't help. I didn't say anything to him about it, but chose to let Albert deal with the situation instead. Black was surprised when he realized that I knew what he was doing. He must have thought a white woman was innocent and would never suspect what he was doing. He didn't know that I, unfortunately, learned about drugs at a young age.

Another time, I smelled something that reminded me of burnt hair. I looked out the back window to see what appeared to be a cat in the fire. I could tell by the shape of the body even though the hair was gone. Black had killed a cat and was roasting it in the backyard. I shouted at Black asking him, "Why did you kill that cat?"

He told me that the cat got caught in the rattrap he put in the compound to catch the big rats. I was not only disgusted, but also heartbroken for that cat. In America, it is a crime to harm cats or dogs, let alone eat them. But in some parts of Nigeria it is simply another source of meat. Other times Black roasted large rats. He also sold some of these rats for others to eat. I was disgusted.

Albert warned Black not to even let me see him slaughter the chicken we would eat for dinner. I had never seen a live chicken being butchered. Albert knew I would not be able to eat the meal if I saw it.

Trying to communicate with Black was very difficult for both of us in the beginning. He spoke Pidgin English and Hausa while I spoke American English. I asked him if the security guard was around. "He done go," he said.

I thought he meant, *He don't go*. "Okay, go and call him," I said.

"Madam, he done go," He said.

I was confused and ended the conversation in frustration. Later I told Albert about our misunderstanding. He assured me that when someone says "he done go," that means that he has gone. Pidgin English was confusing! Another time he came through the back door and said, "Mommy, I want to chop!"

"What do you mean you want to chop? You want to chop wood?" I asked.

"No, I want to eat!" he said as he moved his jaws and teeth together in an eating motion. "In Nigeria it is common to say chop instead of eat," he explained. I explained to him, "In America chop usually means to chop some wood with an axe or something."

Eventually, we grew to understand each other very well. However, in the beginning, I did not like it at all when he called me "Mommy." "I asked him, "Why do you keep calling me Mommy, because I am not your Mommy. I only have one child!" He was just as old as I was, if not older. I later found out that he was calling me Mommy out of respect. In Nigerian culture, younger people call the elders Mommy or Daddy or to show respect for someone that is in a higher position. It is considered disrespectful to call people by their first name, so everybody becomes Mommy, Daddy, Auntie, or Uncle.

In this culture, women with children are called "Mama" followed by their first child's name. Most of the time, I was called "Mama Whitney." This, too, was a sign of respect. I always preferred to be called by the name that my mother gave to me, but I accepted the cultural nickname. Many men are called "Baba," which means "father," but has the implication of old age or experience. It is considered a great honor to be old in Nigeria.

Black would often come to the back door saying, "kong kong." When Albert came home, I asked, "Why does Black keep telling me, 'kong kong!'"He laughed at me again. "It means knock knock!"

On July 23, 2006, Whitney turned 6 years old. We invited people over to celebrate. Black was supposed to be helping us with the preparation, but he was so hung over he could barely move. The room he slept in reeked of vomit. He needed to fetch many buckets of water for me, but it took him an hour just to get one bucketful. We didn't realize he had a drinking problem until that day. We tried to help him and give him advice. We suspected he had friends among the local people who had graduated from college only to discover that there were no jobs for them. The idle time and lack of occupation caused them to make many unwise choices, and Black joined right in on their escapades.

Black had a wife back home in his village, and he also had two children by two different women. He was not willing to change or try to make use of the opportunity he had with us. He went to his village numerous times without informing us. He also refused to listen to instructions.

Albert's father had told us not to drink the well water without boiling and filtering it because we could get typhoid fever. He explained to us that it was safer to buy pure water or bottled water.

To ensure that we would not get any water-born diseases, we had to boil our water, let it cool, put it through a filter and put it into bottles. This seemed like a lot of work, but it was necessary for our health. I told Black, "Help me fill the bottles, I will be back soon."

This meant that he would have to put the water inside the filter and allow enough time for it to pass through the filter. By the time I came back, he had already filled every bottle in the house and I knew that there was no way that he could have had enough time to complete the job as instructed. I was so annoyed and afraid that he had put some dirty well water in those bottles.

I was pregnant and angry, so I asked him, "Do you want us to die?" Eventually I told Black to return to his village.

After quite some time we also got tired of filtering the water, so we started buying pure water. That solved the problem. After being in Nigeria for nearly five years, we finally bought a water dispenser.

During that time we didn't even have running water in the house. We finally found a plumber to put a pump in the well. Albert had paid a plumber to do the job before we came to Nigeria. However, the man was paid before the job was finished and he never showed up to complete the process. We tried another plumber a few years later, but he couldn't get the pump to work. When we finally got running water in the house, the children and I were ecstatic.

Throughout those first five years we also lived without cable TV until I decided that we should introduce Nickelodeon and other cartoon channels to our children for them to enjoy. It was strange to finally have TV to watch after so many years.

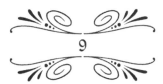

9

I didn't know where to start when it came to cooking in Nigeria. We went into town and I found a can of spaghetti sauce in a "supermarket" (actually a small shop) for 700 naira (about 5 dollars). I cooked the can of sauce with spaghetti and gave it to some family cousins who had come to visit. They had a horrible time trying to eat the sauce because the spices were so different from what they normally ate. My American family tended to eat more bland foods while Albert's Nigerian family enjoyed lots of hot pepper.

Later on I discovered that I could get a huge quantity of tomatoes much cheaper and could make my own sauce, better known as "stew" by the Nigerians. I washed the tomatoes in water and sent them to a woman near the house who would process them in her grinding machine. She earned her living by grinding tomatoes for people in the neighborhood, collecting no more than 100 naira (60 cents) at one time, depending on how many tomatoes there were to be ground.

Children usually took the tomatoes to the lady for me, since there were always children around the neighborhood willing to run errands. One day as I stood near a grinding machine, I noticed how filthy it was. I asked if that was where they usually sent my tomatoes to be ground.

They said, "No, there is another woman that is a bit cleaner." I was relieved, because if we had become sick, I would have known why. Not only was the woman's grinding machine filthy, the bucket was literally black from not being washed and from so many tomatoes being ground into the bucket. I had a clean bucket in my house that I wanted to give her, hoping that she could see the difference in the clean one compared to the dirty one.

One of the children took it over to her for me and I told him to ask her for the dirty one. When he brought it back, I cleaned it with an "iron sponge" (steel wool) and sent it back to her. The boy told me that she laughed when he returned the bucket to her. My mother taught me that it doesn't matter how little money you have, it's no reason to be filthy. However, my goal of helping her was not well received. The next time she saw me; she gave me an angry look and didn't say one word. Since greetings are important in Nigeria, that was unusual. My good intentions had offended her.

My desire was to learn how to make my husband's favorite soup to please him. Eventually I learned how to make red stew, egusi soup, fried rice, yam porridge and jollof/fried rice—all common dishes in Nigeria. I also learned how to improvise in order to make foods that were familiar to me. Thankfully, Albert settled for whatever I cooked as long as I was happy.

Still I continually craved the American foods that were familiar to me. Some people enjoy trying new foods, while others stick with what is usual to them, and they feel lost when they don't have the foods they recognize. I have difficulty eating something that does not taste good or is not familiar to me, while Albert can eat just about anything, even if he doesn't like it.

Several Nigerians told me that I had to learn to eat their foods; but I knew they would have a hard time eating biscuits and gravy or macaroni and cheese (a common American dish) if I served it to them. In fact, I gave Black some mashed potatoes one day. He said "Ewww! What is this? I wouldn't eat this if I was about to die of starvation." I wasn't offended but completely understood that it was foreign to him. That was exactly how I felt about some Nigerian dishes.

One day I discovered that I had all the ingredients to make a banana cake. I made it and was happy to sit down and eat this very familiar food. It gave me comfort.

I became weary of having nothing to do. I complained to Albert, "I cannot continue to just sit here every day looking at the walls!" He suggested that I could make banana bread to sell at nearby shops. I did that for a while, but I began to lose interest because the profit was not very great. I only did it in the first place to keep myself busy. Adjusting to the food was the biggest problem I experienced while living in Nigeria. I found comfort in eating foods that I ate as a child. Many times I made long lists of what I would like to get from home, without any idea of how I would get any of it. I can remember hoarding any food that I enjoyed because I was afraid somebody would eat it all and I wouldn't have it later. I told Albert that I wished someone could just inject me with food so I felt full and I wouldn't have to worry about how it tasted.

Fried potatoes were the closest thing to comfort food that I could get since they reminded me of French fries. I ate them every single day for lunch nearly the entire time I lived in Nigeria—for eight years! That is no exaggeration. Not because there was no food, but because of the type of food available. Finally, after learning how to bake cakes and cookies from scratch, I baked all of the time, to the degree that people thought that was all Americans eat.

One time when my brother-in-law and his wife came to visit, we all went to church together and had plans to go to their father's house to eat. Before we went over there, we stopped at our house so I could make some tuna patties for Whitney and me because I knew we wouldn't to be able to eat what they were cooking. My brother-in-law's wife didn't understand why I was preparing this food. After I made the tuna patties, she came in the kitchen and took some while asking her husband if he wanted some.

That frustrated me because we were left with only two or three patties for Whitney and me. My sister-in-law totally missed the point of why I was making something that Whitney and I could eat: it was so we wouldn't be looking at them eating their Nigerian soups while we had empty stomachs. That happened often until I learned to eat a few new things, like fried yam or plantain.

Many times I drank an entire pitcher of sweet tea throughout the day trying to kill the cravings that I had to eat something familiar. That came from the habit of growing up in America and being used to snacking all day too.

Going to the market was an unpleasant chore to me. Albert had to teach me how to shop in Nigeria. We must bargain for every item we buy, otherwise we will end up paying the "first price" the seller asks, which is often much higher than the going price. The market became like a game to me. If I wanted to buy something in the open market, I would approach the vendor and ask them, "How much?" The seller would ask, "How much you go pay?" in Pidgin English. Then the bargain process would begin. I dreaded the extra time it took to bargain, so I often begged my husband to shop for us. He could always get it cheaper as long as they didn't see me and my white skin, which often made things cost more. Sometimes he stepped out of the car to buy something while we waited in the car. At the beginning I wondered why it was taking so long just to buy one item, until I understood the bargaining process.

When I went to the market without Albert, I could bargain like an average Nigerian. The women in the market would always be surprised when I would drag the price low. I would tell them what I was going to pay and refuse to relent. Other times I would become frustrated. Some Nigerians believe that being white automatically means the person is rich and should be able to pay "first price." Sometimes I would explain to them that my being a white person doesn't mean I have plenty of money. I would tell them that I am not a missionary, I am not making dollars, and I make all my money in Nigeria. Sometimes I wondered why I even spent time trying to explain, but I did it because I lived on a modest budget and I had to spend my funds carefully in the first few years. We lived on 25,000 naira a month, which is about 150 dollars. This helped me relate to Nigerians and how they live. Many people told me how they felt very comfortable around me. We can't reach out to people if we cannot relate to them, and my circumstances helped me in this area.

Another frustration came from having to buy meat covered with flies. It smelled horrific after sitting in the sun all day. I went with Albert once to get "minced meat" (ground beef) from the Abattoir market and was disgusted by the looks and smells of the open butchery. I saw a man slapping what they call the "towel" of the cow, onto the ground. I soon stopped eating beef altogether. Thankfully, I have never been much of a meat eater.

When it came time to look for a school for Whitney, Albert and I drove around town looking at different options. We happened to find a school close to our house. Later we heard that it was one of the best schools in Jos, and it did turn out to be a very good school. However, after a few years the quality of the school started to deteriorate, yet the proprietress continued to raise the school fees every year. We paid a computer fee even though Whitney never once used a computer. Every parent was asked to pay a fee that would enable the school to dig a borehole to get running water, but we never did see a borehole. However, we did see the owner of the school come to work with a brand new Peugeot and then later a brand new Honda.

Owning a school in Nigeria is a profitable business because there is a need for good quality education since the government has failed at that. Often people who have the money to start a school do it just for the money and fail to focus on the future of the children and the impact it will have on their lives.

We prayed about leaving the school and eventually put Whitney in another school in the neighboring community of Rayfield. That meant we had to drive a long distance to take her to school and pick her up again each day, but it was worth the effort. We never had any complaints about the school, which was run by a woman from the UK who was also married to a Nigerian.

When Whitney finished Grade 5, it was time to search for a secondary school since that school only had elementary classes. All those years while Whitney was in school I felt rather comfortable about the condition of the schools and the quality of the education. One day when Albert and I went searching for a suitable secondary school, I had this overwhelming feeling of wanting to go back to America because there were not enough options in Jos. The secondary school campuses were not a pretty sight. As we drove into the compound of the school that we were considering, I immediately looked at Albert and said, "Oh my goodness, no way, turn around." I wanted to weep because of the way I felt about my daughter having to go to school there. Apparently there are nicer schools in other part of Nigeria like Abuja or Lagos.

We learned that this school was the only one that gave the option of going to day school, while all the other secondary schools required students to board at the school. There was no way I was going to allow my daughter to leave home and go to boarding school. We had no choice but to take her there. I was afraid for her having to go there and I never once went inside her school. I couldn't bear the pain. I thought I would just feel worse if I went inside and saw the conditions. I never expressed my feelings to Whitney because I didn't want to subject her to my negative views of her school. I did not want to face reality. Fortunately, she did well and took First Position each term in her first year.

One day she came home crying and showed me a mark on her hand saying that the teacher had whipped her and everybody else in the class because of what one student had done. I asked her what he used to beat her with and she said he used a wire. I wanted to tell her that I was sorry, not solely because she got beat by her teacher, but sorry that she had to go to that school. Instead I chose not to tell her how I really felt. I wept that night and felt so horrible inside for what she had to face in her school. I just wanted my child to go to a civilized school: a school with running water, clean painted walls, and to have extracurricular activities.

As tears rolled down my face, I spoke to Albert and pleaded with him to go talk to the principal of the school informing him that nobody should touch Whitney like that. There are more proper ways to punish a child. The principal told Albert that he would have a talk with the teacher. After all, the school had given us a list of rules and punishments during registration, and we spoke to Whitney to make sure she obeyed them so that she would not be punished in an uncivil way.

Whitney also had to wash the toilets in her school where there was no running water. I decided that it would just help her to be a grateful child. In the end, she will be more educated as to what happens in other parts of the world. I also realized that no journey or circumstance lasts forever.

I later began to look at the bright side of things. Even though Whitney was not going to the finest looking school in Nigeria, she was learning about Jesus in the school, unlike in America where prayers and Jesus Christ had been taken out of the school system. I also felt she would not be influenced by drugs, sex, and alcohol like many other children her age are exposed to in America. I decided that I would rather have her get beaten on the hand than be exposed to worldly influences.

I slowly began to see the good in our journey to Nigeria instead of the bad.

After just a few months, I became weary and tired. I felt like I had seen enough of Nigeria and just wanted to go back home to my own country. I had a ticket to return in June since I was only supposed to be there for six months. We thought we would all be able to go back to America, but we were halted by the immigration process. I often told Albert that I couldn't wait until June came so I could go back home.

I would get very upset telling Albert, "I hate this country and there is no way I will stay another day."

Albert would shout back at me saying, "This is the best life you have ever had!"

After awhile, I calmed down. I had to decide which was best: my comfort or the future of my children and our marriage. As more time passed, I asked myself, *Where is home?* My mother had died and my family members and my father didn't show much interest in me. As I reflected back on my past life, I accepted the reality of what Albert was telling me. I no longer had running water, American food, consistent electricity, and all of the other comforts; but those were not the important things in life. The eight years I lived in Nigeria became the most stable life I ever had, learning more in my entire life than ever before.

I called my aunt and asked her to please send me a package of things that I enjoyed eating, like macaroni and cheese and Jiffy Cornbread. She did send it, but it took three months to get there; and all of the items smelled and tasted like the fuel from the airplane or the ship. Even so, I was grateful that someone back home took the effort for me. That was the first and last package she sent to me since it cost so much for the postage.

Another aunt sent packages frequently at first, but that eventually stopped. After we were in Nigeria for several years, my stepmother became generous and thoughtful enough to send us things. We always felt like children on Christmas Day when we got a package from America. It gave us something to look forward to when we knew something would be coming.

I always wished that my family members would have challenged themselves enough to learn how to call Nigeria, but I never once received a phone call from them. It hurt me deeply, but God healed those wounds. He brought some great people in my life that would help heal that pain.

As much as I wanted to go back, I had to realize that if I left Nigeria, I would be right back to how I felt when I was away from my husband. I would also end up being a single mother. Plus, I would be derailing God's plan for my life. Another question I asked myself was, *Where would I live if I went back?*

I had no answers to my questions. I had nowhere to go. There wasn't one place I could think of where I could go and feel accepted. If I left, our children would grow up not knowing their father. I did not want my decisions to be the reason why they did not get a chance to be raised by him. I did not want my children to grow up in a broken home like I did. I also did not want to leave my husband behind.

So June came and went, and I stayed in Nigeria.

10

Early in our time in Jos, we began to look for a church. The first one we attended was named Living Faith, a rather large church, and I was not happy there. I couldn't understand what the preacher was saying and the loudspeakers were deafening—a common thing in Nigeria. I also did not like the way people would stare at me. I never got used to the constant stares of the people looking at how white I was. I would often hear someone shout in their various languages: "Oyibo"(Yoruba), "Baturia" (Hausa) or "Onye-öcha" (Igbo). Each of those meant "white person." I avoided weddings and burials because it made me so uncomfortable. I would wish I was a tortoise and could go inside my shell.

The one time I did go to a burial in my mother-in-law's village of Ganawuri, I felt as if the entire village was looking at me. Anytime I was in a situation like that, I would be ready to go back to America. Many times I would feel someone reach out and touch me or touch my hair because they were curious about me.

When I was a child, my mother taught me not to stare or point at people, so I couldn't understand how they could be so rude to stare at me like that. They were simply curious and happy to see a foreigner in their country, and it was never meant to be offensive or derogatory.

One day we were driving down the road and I looked over and saw some white people. I was excited and curious as to what they were doing in Nigeria. Albert explained that they were missionaries. They were attending the chapel service at the missionary school in Jos. I was thrilled that there were many American missionaries living right in Jos. I felt a load of isolation being lifted from me.

We attended the chapel service. There I met three women; individually they invited our family over for dinner. Two of the women were also married to Nigerians. The first question I asked one of the women was if she knew how to make cornbread in Nigeria. I was so hungry for cornbread with butter like my mother used to make. From this friend I learned that cornbread was made from ground corn. I had to buy the dried kernels of corn, take them to be ground, and mix it with flour, sugar, eggs, and oil. I was shocked and felt ignorant. I never really knew how to cook from scratch; in America we just bought it in a box, mixed it up and baked it.

After living in Nigeria for a few years, I became close friends with Mary Beth Oyebade. She helped me in so many ways, like where to get things that the average American would want, where to find different shops in town where I could get special things that came from America or things that were just different from what we would find in an open market. I never had a friend like her in my entire life. She often brought me things that she knew would brighten my day as she knew how much I missed home.

On my first birthday in Nigeria, Mary Beth came to my house and said she was taking me somewhere, but I had to put on a blindfold. She took me to the Baptist Hostel where I could enjoy a hot shower because she knew how much I missed taking showers and how frustrated I was with taking my baths from a bucket. She had invited some other people my age and made tacos and cheese dip, which was my favorite food. She contributed to my resilience.

During any event in our life, Mary Beth and her husband, Bayo, were there to show they cared in many ways. Just as she encouraged me, her Nigerian husband befriended Albert and encouraged him. Bayo was from the Yoruba tribe just as Albert was, and Albert always felt like he could talk with him about anything. Mary Beth and Bayo were a bit older than us and could offer advice.

When summertime came and Hillcrest School was on break, many missionaries went to their home countries, so there was no Sunday service in the chapel. We decided we had to look for a church for our family. One Sunday as we drove around, we came across a church close to Hillcrest School named Evangel Chapel. We started attending there, and it was at this church that I gave my life to Christ and both Albert and I grew in the Lord.

I remember that day like no other. I cried and let out all of the pain, fear, and frustrations that had been building inside me for so long. It was the beginning of having all my burdens being lifted from me. I was ready for God to heal my mind and my heart. I needed Him and He was ready for me. I had never really mourned the death of my mother. I was in so much pain, but God lifted me and took away all the pain that I had ever gone through. I felt as if I was floating in the air, my heart felt so much lighter. I felt like I could rest because He carried away all of my burdens.

At this church I met many Christians and missionaries who became great role models in my life. It felt like coming home each time we drove into the compound of the church. There we met two American boys who were twins. Their father was the Pastor of the church and he was also President of the seminary connected to the church. He happened to be an American who had come to Nigeria almost a decade before we got there. Their family had such a huge impact on our lives during the beginning of our walk with the Lord, which was a very important time. They are Scott and LaVonna Ennis and their three children, Jonathan, Jordan, and Johanna.

To this day, I believe that it was a part of God's plan for us to become members of this church and to meet the Ennis family along with the rest of the members of that church. They were constantly thinking of us and helping in any way that they could. They did countless things for us. I know they were God-sent because they never really knew just how much we struggled during those times, yet they always helped us at times when we needed help most. God was working through them and others to reach us.

God had sent me to Nigeria and placed these two wonderful women in my life to be such great role models for me, to make up for my childhood of growing up with a mother that didn't teach me how to be a woman.

One day LaVonna told me her mother had taught her that a woman is supposed to make the home a place where her husband and her children will look forward to coming home. That stuck in my head and I learned from it. I thought about our home and wondered if my husband enjoyed coming home. I strived to make sure the house was always clean, dinner was cooked, the kids were clean, and everything was in order. And Albert always did seem to look forward to coming home.

When Whitney's birthday came, I invited LaVonna's daughter to come for a sleepover party. At that time LaVonna did not know us very well, so she did not allow Johanna to sleep over, but she did bring her to the party. I learned from her that I cannot allow my children to go for sleepovers when I do not know the person well enough. I have to make sure that other people will not influence my child in a negative way.

LaVonna's husband, Reverend Ennis, spoke to us during a sermon saying that we should control what we watch and what we listen to because it can affect our relationship and our walk with Jesus. I went home and threw out every CD that was not appropriate. Now I speak to my children about choosing wisely the music and the movies they watch, telling them that we have to be careful about what we allow into our minds. If the words of the song are not positive words then we shouldn't listen to it.

Sometime later, LaVonna and Reverend Ennis were going to travel and needed someone to take care of their children. They asked Albert if we would mind staying with their children in their house for a week. I felt honored that they would choose us; it meant that God had truly changed our lives.

By July, 2006, we had been in Nigeria for six months and I was pregnant. When our baby boy was born the following April, we named him Micah Babatunde Owonubi. Babatunde means "daddy has come back" in the Yoruba language. I will explain later why we decided to give him that name.

Albert went to work each day, so I would sit in our house alone every day with no electricity. Sometimes I would ask him to drop me at his father's house where there were other people to talk to. They never knew what to make for me to eat, but I would tell them to just make chips for me. My father-in-law's house on Apata Street always seemed to be hotter than our house. I could make do without having an air conditioner in my house on Wamba Road, but always felt like I was going to suffocate in that house. My father-in-law had an air conditioner in his parlor, but the power never stayed on long enough to keep it cool.

Sometimes my father-in-law would come home from the office and find me in his house, so we would sit and talk to each other. Well, he would talk to me and I would listen. He was a lonely man after the death of his wife and I enjoyed the chance to spend time with him. He was an emotionally sensitive man. One time he told me a story about his deceased wife. In return I told him about my deceased mother and we both ended up in tears. It was a painful time, but a great moment to experience with the father of the man that I had married and loved so much.

My father-in-law was always concerned about me and he showed it in many ways. He bought a one-hundred-pound bag of potatoes for me since he noticed that I liked to eat them. Another time he once asked Albert, "Why are you speaking Hausa when you know your wife cannot understand?" My father–in–law was such a thoughtful man and he made living in Nigeria easier for me. He had traveled out of the country before, so he understood how it was for someone being in a foreign country.

It is the culture of Nigeria for me to call my father-in-law "Daddy." At first, it felt odd for me. It had been so many years since I called my own father Daddy, so just the thought of saying the name "Daddy" brought painful memories from my childhood. However, it wasn't long before I was calling him "Daddy," and felt honored to do so.

Christmas was approaching and my father-in-law told everyone he was going to his village of Ogidi, and he wanted all of us to join him for New Year's. Even though I was six months pregnant and already had swollen feet, I decided it would be good for us to travel to his village six hours away. It would be nice to change environments and see something different. Visiting a village would be a unique experience. One of Albert's relatives was worried about me and asked him, "What will your wife eat? The oven doesn't work in the village." I appreciated his concern, and I brought along some cans of tuna and sweet corn as well as some potatoes. I wanted to make sure that I didn't get stuck eating anything I did not want to eat.

When we arrived at the five-bedroom family house in Ogidi, we were hot, sweaty, and dusty. We all wanted to bathe, so the younger ones went to fetch water from the well. They found that the water was brown since it was low from months without rain. We had the choice to bathe with the brown water or to continue to be hot, sweaty, and dusty. It was a rather hard decision to make, but I chose to bathe with the dirty water.

We had been there for three days when we heard a knock at our bedroom door in the middle of night. I was tired because of my pregnancy and from being in a room with no lock where people were going in and out all day. I couldn't believe someone was knocking on the door at that time of night. I tapped Albert to wake him up so he could answer the door. Talatu said something in Hausa, and the only word I understood was "daddy." I knew something was wrong with Daddy.

We all rushed into the room and saw him lying on his bed with his eyes open, not breathing. I touched his arm and when I felt no pulse, I began to cry. I looked up at my husband and wanted to wrap my arms around him and take away all the pain of losing his father. The whole house was awake by this time since we all started shouting and crying. My brother-in-law and his wife were there as well. My brother-in-law called a nearby pastor to come and pray in the middle of the night. We were all praying in the bedroom together while our daddy lay on the bed unmoving. They prayed that he would come back to life. I knew there was power in prayer, but something made me wonder why we were not rushing him to the hospital. However, he had already died and the nearest hospital was too far away.

It was as if my father-in-law knew he was going to die, and he wanted to die in his village. I had only spent one year with him, but I was grateful to have had that time. If I hadn't come to Nigeria, I would never have had the privilege of getting to know him. If Albert had not been deported from America, he wouldn't have spent those last days with his father. My heart ached for my husband and his siblings. They had already lost their mother in 2003, and now their father was gone. Their mother saw three of the grandchildren, while their father saw four of the grandchildren. Today there are thirteen grandchildren.

My heart ached realizing he was gone. My father-in-law brought me such great joy in the time I knew him; I thoroughly enjoyed spending time with him. I loved how he was so considerate of me and he understood the difficulty I had living in a strange land. I was sad that my children would grow up without grandparents. I was also devastated that I would continue to live in Nigeria without my father-in-law or mother-in-law. At the same time, I knew my American family didn't give us support like our friends and family did in Nigeria.

My father-in-law did not get to see our son. When he was born, our son looked just like his grandfather. In Nigerian culture, it is expected that the child will be given a name with its meaning from the tribe of that person. So we named him Micah *Babatunde* Owonubi, meaning "Daddy has come back." The name fit him well.

11

Soon after that Christmas in the village, Mary Beth, whom I had met at Hillcrest Chapel, offered me a job since she knew I didn't have much to do. I worked from 8 a.m. to noon at Mashiah Foundation, a nonprofit organization helping women and children affected by HIV/AIDS. Mary Beth had moved to Nigeria when she was 26 years old, but she had dreamed of working in Africa since she was 16. She enjoyed making quilts, so her husband suggested that she show the women how to sew. The women in their organization are taught sewing techniques and are given sewing projects every week, and the money they earn enables them to support themselves. My job was to supervise the quality control of the women's sewing projects which would be put in the shop and sold to visitors.

Every day I walked to the sewing center from my house, which was not too far, but far enough to help me get exercise while I was pregnant. I worked there until my delivery date was near. While there I met two lovely ladies, among many others, who were infected with HIV. When I found out they could not read, I invited them to come to my house twice a week for reading lessons. I enjoyed teaching these women who were so eager to learn.

By the time I was nine months pregnant, it was the hottest time of the year. There was often no electricity in the night so we couldn't use the fan to give us some relief from the heat. It was just too expensive to run the generator all night. The mosquito net we used to cover our bed seemed to block any small breeze we might catch. In the middle of one hot night, we decided to remove it. There we were tearing it down with great excitement. It was as if somebody had been forcing us to sleep inside it. I would become so hot that I would take several cold baths in the night to cool off. I just seemed hotter afterwards. Eventually, I would sit up in my bed and just cry, feeling hopeless and frustrated because of the heat.

In addition to the heat, our neighbor's dog would bark all night. That also kept me from getting a good night's sleep. Then there were the sounds of babies crying, the neighbors pounding ingredients in a mortar to make soup, and conversations from the nearby neighbors early in the morning. There were all kinds of unfamiliar sounds that became a part of my existence.

I would shout out my bedroom window telling the dog to shut up. I'm sure the neighbors thought the white woman next door was crazy, while I wondered how the owners of the dog and the other neighbors could sleep through the night. Amazingly, after I delivered my baby, I never heard that dog again.

The first time I heard prayers at 4:00 in the morning, I had no idea what it was. It sounded like someone was shouting very slowly, "It is time to wake up!" Albert told me that it was the Muslims praying from their mosque. After what happened on 9/11 in America, I was a bit frightened since I had never heard Muslims praying while growing up in Bauxite, Arkansas.

Frequently, the neighbors would have a party on a school night and would play music extremely loud until 2:00 in the morning. They were directly next door with only the compound wall separating us, and when they played their music it sounded as if they were in my bedroom. It drove me nuts because I couldn't sleep until they decided that the party was over. There are no laws against such disturbances in Nigeria.

It was almost time to deliver and I was afraid of the pain of the childbirth since I had an epidural when Whitney was born and felt no pain at all. Albert had asked me if I wanted to go home to America and deliver the baby, but it seemed like a better option to have my baby in Nigeria where my husband could be with me in the delivery room. It also would have cost a lot more money to fly home and pay the hospital bill in America. The entire hospital bill in Nigeria only cost us around 20,000 naira (125 dollars), plus the items that we were asked to buy for cleaning up after the delivery. It was all so odd to me. I was especially shocked when they told us to bring our own hot water to use for bathing after the delivery, and to bring our own food as well.

My American missionary doctor had assured me she would give me some good pain medication. But by the time I asked her for it, she said it was too late to take anything because it might interfere with the delivery of the baby. I wondered why in the world she didn't give it to me in time. I ended up delivering my baby without any pain medications at all, not even Tylenol. I didn't even cry and I felt like I had just received my certificate for becoming a real African woman since that is how Nigerian women have their babies, unless it is a C-section.

By 3:00 in the morning, April 3, 2007, I delivered my 8-pound baby boy. We were grateful to God for no complications during the childbirth and I was released from the hospital ten hours later. I had heard many sad stories of women in Nigeria dying during childbirth along with the baby; so when a woman gives birth with no complications, it is even more reason to give glory to God.

The hospital was so hot, and the nurses would not allow me to turn the fan on for the fear of the baby getting sick. That is a common belief of Nigerians—they feel that a baby has to be kept very warm and bundled up. I was irritated by this belief, which meant that I had to keep wiping the sweat from my forehead. The temperature outside was at least 90 degrees Fahrenheit. People would ask us why we didn't put a cap on the baby's head. We would respond nicely by telling them that it was not cold outside.

It was normal for Nigerian women in Jos to wrap their babies in several layers of clothing, regardless of how hot it is outside. Along with several layers of clothes, the baby would also be covered with a blanket. I heard of some babies dying from being smothered with so many layers in the heat. The more enlightened and educated Nigerians know that colds and other illnesses are caused by viruses and germs. I also think some people just didn't know the difference between putting a cap on the baby in the rainy season when it can be a bit cold and not putting one in the dry season when it is hot. And some women would never give their baby or child a drink of cold water either.

People even told me that my baby would get sick because I was eating or drinking cold things during pregnancy. There was no way that I was going to deprive my baby or myself from anything cold knowing how hot it was outside. The average American enjoys cold drinks even when it is cold outside. And we deliver our babies in the air conditioning. We also drink cold drinks after the delivery and I have never heard of anyone falling sick because of it. The Nigerian women I knew were told to drink lots of hot water after the childbirth. After I gave birth, I would have loved to have had a cold drink. In fact, to find a cold drink was often a luxury. Micah hardly ever had colds and he enjoyed drinking cold drinks. The babies that always had a cap on their head and wore many layers of clothes seemed to be sick more often.

Soon after delivering a baby, some Nigerian women are bathed by their own mother or aunt, who presses hot water on their body. I made it very clear that nobody was going to come and bathe me! I could bathe myself without any help. I didn't need a severely hot bath when the weather was already hot enough outside.

Many people were surprised that I was strong immediately after having the baby. I went to church one week after Micah was born. They didn't expect me to attend that quickly since it is normal for the woman to stay indoors for forty days or three months, depending on the tribe.

Some women learn how to care for their children from their mothers, and every culture and family has different practices. One custom in Nigeria is to hold an infant by the arm or leg and throw it in the air during bath time to make the baby strong. I witnessed that when I saw my brother-in-law's wife bathing her baby. I sat there with my mouth wide open in amazement. I thought that she was being mean to the baby and told Albert about it. He was unaware of this practice and planned to speak to his brother about it. From that experience, I made it clear that I would be bathing my baby myself; and Albert made sure everyone respected my wishes.

When I came home from the hospital, people came to greet us and to see the newest member of the family. My neighbors in the slums next door saw us driving to our gate and were so excited. This is one of my favorite parts of the culture in Nigeria—when friends, neighbors, church members, and family members came to share in joy or sorrow, for a birth, a wedding or a death in the family. Those who didn't come to the house would phone to show respect. This was very unlike my family in America, who never called when I gave birth to my son or even when we had a death in the family.

In the beginning it would stress me out when people would pop in unexpectedly, but I began adjusting to this custom. It was nice to have guests in the house. With all the struggles and hardships of living in Nigeria, it's the people that make it such a great country. People care about each other, unlike my experiences in the western part of the world where people seem to only care for themselves.

We dedicated our baby in Evangel Chapel Assembly of God, and felt honored for Reverend Scott Ennis to dedicate our son to the Lord. Our baby was just two weeks old. All of our friends came to help us celebrate our joy. The women in the church lined up outside the church dressed in their beautiful Nigerian wrappers, dancing toward the altar. LaVonna Ennis led the group, dancing down the aisle with our baby in her arms. She often spoke about how much she enjoyed dancing with the babies in the church to present them before the Lord for dedication.

Albert wanted me to dress up in Nigerian attire on the day of the dedication when we would stand in front of the whole church to give our testimony of the birth of our baby. My outfit of Nigerian lace had a long-sleeved oversized top. The skirt was sewn more like a small bed sheet meant to be wrapped around the waist and tied in a knot in the back. I wore the same lace cloth that was bought for me during the burial of our "daddy." It is common for many of the friends and relatives to wear clothes made from the same fabric during weddings and burials.

While it is exciting to wear the elaborate traditional attire and everyone said I looked beautiful in it, I couldn't wait to get home and get it off because I felt like I was in a strait-jacket. I did grow to love Nigerian fabrics and would often have a new style sewn.

When it came time to breastfeed my baby, I went outside to the car so that nobody could watch me. Some women in Nigeria freely breastfeed their babies, regardless of who is looking or where they are. I felt like people already stared at me enough, so I didn't want to draw any more attention to myself. Once again I felt like someone in a strait-jacket because it was so difficult to struggle with the clothes while my baby was crying to be fed.

After the dedication we invited many family members and church members to come and eat in our house. This is a common practice. I was happy to see so many people sharing in the joy of the new birth in our family. The church had also been filled to overflowing at the dedication, and all the church members stood in front of the church with us to show support. I had never experienced such love and care by so many people in all my life!

Shortly after giving birth, Albert invited a family member named Grace to our house to stay and help me with the baby and the housework. This is also typical in the culture of Nigeria. Americans, when we have our babies, are left to do everything without much help since most people are busy trying to make their own living. However, it is less stressful in America since there is running water, electricity, and washing machines. In Nigeria, the mother or a younger girl from the village will come to assist.

Grace attended school at the Polytechnic and ended up living with us for three years until she got married. She was one of the many other cousins that grew up in the Apata Street house with my husband's family. Grace became like a sister to me.

When Micah was just a year old, some spots appeared on his back that looked like they could have been measles or chicken pox. We were not certain since we hadn't experienced either illness. We took Micah to the doctor and he couldn't tell us what it was, but he gave us some calamine lotion and told us to come back in a few days if it hadn't gone away by then. When we put the calamine lotion on Micah's back, he would scream because of the pain. We still had no idea what was causing the pain. We just wanted to help our baby and for the pain to cease.

A few days passed and the spots worsened. We chose not to go back to that doctor since he had been of no help. We did not sleep for nearly a week because Micah would wake up in the night crying because of his extreme discomfort. We just hoped it was going to get better, whatever it was. Sunday morning came and Albert and Whitney went to church while I stayed home with Micah. When they arrived back home after church, Albert said he had told the Pastor's wife about the spots on Micah's back, and she told him what it was and what to do. We were so relieved that our baby would finally relief from this condition.

The Pastor's wife said Micah had mango worms. We were to put Vaseline on the tip of each spot. Then the worm would stick his head out to get air and we would be able to squeeze it out. I felt like I was about to faint hearing about the worms in my baby boy's back. It might have been different if there were just a few, but we squeezed thirty-four mango worms out of his back!

Albert said he was going to get them out all at once so that Micah could rest. He laid Micah down on the couch to start the process and I walked out of the house saying, "Oh Jesus, I can't watch this, I can't watch my baby scream in pain!" Then I immediately walked back in the house saying, "Oh Jesus, I can't leave him here and not be with him through his pain!" Tears rushed down my face as the first worm came out of his back. I felt like I was in as much pain as my son was. At the very least, I wished I could take his place so he wouldn't have to deal with the pain.

We used a jam jar to keep all of the worms in one place and to make sure they didn't affect anyone else. We learned that the mango worms lay eggs on clothes that are left outside to dry during the rainy season. When the clothing is worn, the eggs will burrow into the skin and grow into worms. To avoid this we needed to iron all our clothes to kill the eggs.

Just six months after that incident, Micah had an accident in church. I was sick with malaria and Albert and the kids had gone to church. While they were there, a huge speaker fell on Micah in the children's church. I checked Micah and he appeared to be fine, so I didn't worry about it too much. Albert said that another little boy saw the speaker start to fall on Micah and tried to push it out of the way. That boy suffered an injury on his face. I thought, *Wow, what a brave little boy!*

Within just a few hours, Micah began to cry and scream in pain while holding his leg. We looked at it and everything seemed to be okay, but he kept crying. We didn't want to take any chances, so we took him to hospital to have his leg x-rayed. The doctor said that Micah's bone was chipped and he would need a cast on his leg. With the cast on, he had to be carried everywhere and spent most of his time lying down. Thank God for the healing of his skin from the worms and for the quick healing of his leg!

The frequent and unexpected power outages became incredibly annoying and stressful to me. Sometimes we wouldn't have electricity for two weeks. I would be in the middle of cooking and the power would go off. I would freak out for the fear of burning the food on the gas stove, not being able to see what I was cooking until Albert could rush out to turn on the generator. Years of waking up in the middle of the night to use the bathroom made me into an expert at feeling my way through the rooms in the dark. I did knock my head on the door a few times, though. I was very frightened when I couldn't see my children in the darkness. The kids would scream and become scared when the lights went out. We tried to console them in the darkness and tell them to stay put until the light came on or Albert could turn the generator on.

We frequently sat around the house without power during the daytime. When it would suddenly come on, everybody would be so excited. It gave people something to look forward to and something to do. Getting ready for church on a Sunday morning was challenging when there was no power. If we didn't plan ahead and iron our clothes, we might have to go to church a bit wrinkled.

The kids outside my gate would shout in excitement when the power came on after being off for many hours, or sometimes days. As soon as the power came on, it was a chance to charge the phones and laptops, warm bath water, iron clothes, or watch television.

Another time Albert's cousin went out to buy something, taking Micah along; and the power had gone off while they were away. When she came back carrying Micah, she thought our sliding glass door was open, and she crashed right through it in the darkness. Micah screamed and I did not know if they were okay. When the generator came on, I was grateful to God that the broken glass did not cut either one of them.

Before we got a generator, Albert worried about Whitney doing her homework in the darkness with only a candle for light. He often suggested that maybe I should just take her back to America. I knew he didn't want us to be separated again; he just didn't want his daughter to live in such a harsh setting. When he was a child twenty years earlier, conditions in Nigeria were not so bad. The country had deteriorated in the intervening years.

12

A few months after my father-in-law passed away, I invited Albert's childhood nanny, Talatu, and her two boys, Jacob and Bulus, to come and live with us. They were living in the house with my father-in-law, but the situation in the house declined after his death. I greatly respected her because she took care of my husband when he was a child.

There was a small apartment in the house next to us that nobody was using. So I painted the place for her and helped her move what few things she owned into that house. However, for the first year, she lived inside my house, even though I had prepared a place for her and had not intended that she would live with us. Her sons were peeing in the room and making the house smell bad. Jacob was always in trouble: cutting the couch with a razor blade, burning the carpet with the boiling ring, or writing on the wall and the floor.

It was overwhelming to have so many people in the house, and to wake up to so much confusion each morning. So I finally told her it was time for her to start living in the house I had prepared for them. She started sleeping there, but would come to our house at 6:00 in the morning and wouldn't leave until time for bed at night. There was never peace in the house with Jacob and Bulus. When her children acted up, Talatu would raise her hand and slap them right across the face or start beating them on the back. I told her several times that this was not the way to discipline a child and that I did not like it. Micah was very young and he was beginning to imitate hitting people on the back like she did.

Her children would often say, "Momma, I want to s***!" She would reply, "Oya, go and s*** now!" I told them that we don't use that word in our house and I did not want my children walking around imitating that speech. Instead, I wanted them to say "poop." It sounded more civil to me.

Talatu helped take care of Albert and his siblings while they were growing up until she got married and had children of her own. When her youngest son was born, her husband died. When her husband died, she moved back with my husband's parents and worked for them. Albert resisted bringing them to our house, but I insisted. I often regretted not listening to him because of the great amount of stress it caused me. Through this experience I learned to listen to his advice.

There was so much hardship surrounding me, but I needed to be wise in the way that I helped others. The more that people helped me, the more I learned to help others as well. I finally stopped worrying about myself and realized that the world is filled with other people. I learned to put other people ahead of myself, while I used to think of how others could help me.

Albert's family has always helped in supporting Talatu financially, which includes paying school fees for her children. She cannot read, write or count money, so she is incapable of earning a living. Her children have always done poorly in school, but at least they have learned more than their mother did.

Albert and I both have tried for many years to help the two boys, but they have refused to take advantage of the opportunity put before them. Children learn directly from their mother and father or the one that spends the majority of time with them. Talatu just couldn't make logical decisions for herself or for her children. We constantly tried to guide them. We tried to ensure that they studied and did their homework after school instead of playing. If they needed help, we were always there to give assistance.

At the end of each school term the boys would come home with failing report cards. The teacher's comments would be: try harder, wake up from your slumber for a better tomorrow, plays too much, and lacks concentration. So we would discipline them by taking away television privileges or even spanking them on occasion. However, Talatu would allow them to watch TV in their house and would be angry because we disciplined them. While it is common in Nigeria for people to discipline other people's children, it is uncommon when a Nigerian woman does not discipline her own children.

Most mothers in Nigeria would be happy to have someone help discipline her children and guide them. They live by the African proverb made popular by Hillary Clinton, "It takes a village to raise a child." Many times I chose to ignore Talatu's ignorance and would do what I could to help those boys realize what would happen if they did not do well in school and learn. The youngest one cried when I attempted to teach him how to read. The school he attended had failed at that but they still gave him schoolwork that required him to read. I tried to help the boys understand they had an opportunity before them that many children would never have. However, they were still children and couldn't possibly understand the seriousness of the situation.

Their mother seemed to be their worst enemy. Yet, for some reason, they seemed to think that we were the wicked ones. I know that someday when they get older they will have a better understanding of what we were trying to do for them.

Jacob and Bulus had no real structure living with their mother. Regardless of our intentions to help, things did not change. Their mother had no more zeal for them to do better than she did for her own life. She is around 50 years old (she is not even sure of her age) and has nothing to show for her life. I asked her to let me teach her how to read or count and she refused. It is easy to see why her children are not developing good character traits. If not for the Owonubi family, these children probably wouldn't have had the chance to even go to school.

At the age of 10 and 13, the boys were still wetting the bed every night, and the whole house reeked of urine. This was a result of lazy parenting. It was stressful and frustrating trying to help these two boys who received no apparent help from their mother.

For the first few years Talatu lived with us, Albert and I provided the food for all of us to eat. I would buy all Nigerian food and we would cook large amounts of food to feed all eight of us in the house. Whatever we cooked at night would also be eaten for breakfast, a common thing in Nigeria, especially in homes where there are many family members to feed. I never wanted to eat breakfast because of the choice of food, so I only drank Milo (hot chocolate) every morning. Many of our friends were surprised that we were so young and taking care of so many people. I used to feel sorry for my husband who worked so hard to feed all of us.

American food is very expensive in Nigeria, so I basically had given up any chances of getting food that I enjoyed since we were now responsible for feeding Talatu and her boys. Many times, I would get so tired of eating rice that I would rather be hungry than to eat it.

My husband's monthly salary would last about two weeks. The remaining weeks of the month would be tough, but God always provided. Still we were considered rich in Nigeria. I knew some Nigerians who only earned between 5,000 and 10,000 naira (35-70 dollars), which carries them through the entire month. I always wondered how they were able to make it with such a small amount of money. It is the grace of God that helps many people in Nigeria survive with the little money they have. The fact that we were eating rice nearly every day was considered a luxury. Many Nigerians eat rice only during birthday parties or at Christmas time. Wealthier people might have it on other days, and there are some very wealthy people in Nigeria.

Eventually I persuaded Talatu to take better care of herself. I told her that she had to get a job, even though she still received money from the family company every month. I still frequently checked on her to make sure they had food to eat. It became like a job or a hobby for me, sharing what food I had with those around who lacked food.

At times I became overwhelmed and wanted to run away because I was sharing my home with so many people, which is something that the average American does not do. Many Americans love their privacy and do not want to be put out of their comfort zone. But where would I run to and who would help those people in our house? This is something that some Nigerian women would not do either; yet my mother-in-law took care of many people in her home, fed them, and put them through school.

Something within me refused to stop worrying about Auntie Talatu and her children. I was putting all of my energy into helping them, but their lives were not changing.

I have to say that I grew to love Talatu and I love her for who she is. I spent my entire time in Nigeria with her and will never forget about her. She was just another part of God's plan in my life.

I also thought about how God wants us to help the widows and the orphans. After volunteering at the Widows Conferences held every year at our church, I learned so much. I may not have had a great impact on the women, but the event always left a great impression on me. It was amazing how people came together to help these widows who arrived by the hundreds to attend. Some of the women traveled long distances to attend the Conference where they were offered free eye exams and glasses, food, accommodations, wrappers, and sometimes cash. But the most important thing of all is that many of them would give their lives to Christ.

The first year I helped at the Conference, I was given the job of registering their names in a book. That job didn't last long because I couldn't spell the names correctly since the names were not English names, and many of the women could not speak English. Finally I just went around taking pictures and helping with the eye exams. The next year I helped the women of the church cook for seven hundred widows. I cut yams, washed plates outside in a big bowl of water, and handed out food to the women.

13

When I decided to go to Nigeria, Albert and I had no idea how we would survive. We just wanted to be together and did not want to be separated. That is the case for many families that get separated because of deportation. Few women are able to follow their husbands to a foreign land, and few couples will stick it out because of the stress involved with the separation, culture shock, and the immigration process. Luckily for us, my husband had family that could help. His mother was commissioner of police and his father was a doctor.

Many people who get deported back to their countries have nothing to go back to. Children may be separated from their mother or father, and it has a long-lasting effect on their lives. I made a solemn decision to stay in Nigeria until we could all immigrate back to America together as a family—no matter how bad the circumstances became. God had chosen me and had a plan for our family. Today I give God all the glory and honor for making it possible for us to be together. He never failed us and was always on time to meet our needs.

I often thought about how I was able to travel all the way to Africa on the little money that I had and was able to survive in Nigeria for several years. That was clearly the handiwork of my true father, Jesus Christ.

It was hard to imagine how it would have felt for Albert to go on with his life without his wife or his daughter if I had not chosen to stay in Nigeria. I could also understand how it would affect my daughter's life to grow up without her father. Little girls need their daddies.

Albert knew that he could work at the security company that his parents owned. Some said I should leave this part of my story out to protect my husband, but I have to say…WHY? What are we protecting? Why can I not tell the full story of our lives and how God has been faithful throughout? My husband and I were 25 years old when this deportation happened to us. We couldn't control how it happened or when it happened, and Albert has given me permission to share this portion of our journey.

Albert is a hard-working and determined man. There is nothing lazy about him. He went to work every morning and did not come back until evening. He was committed to providing for his family. Albert is an intelligent man that knew how to meet people, get odd jobs, and make money to provide. He did everything he possibly could to get jobs outside of the security company and he studied hard to learn more about computer networking, web development, and video editing. He is seen as a respectable, intelligent man. Many people came to him for advice and admired him. He is a dedicated person, serving God in the church by being involved in the Men's Ministry, being elected as the treasurer, and helping the church in the media department. This was a 180-degree turn from the life he lived before coming back to Nigeria.

Those who know Nigeria recognize that it is not easy for many people to make it in this country. We have been blessed to have God help us along the way. This journey was not easy for Albert either, being married to an American woman and trying to give me the comforts I was accustomed to. I didn't come from a rich family, but I was still used to certain comforts that many Nigerians didn't have. I give my utmost respect to my husband for all of the faithful efforts he made for me and for our children through the years. There were times we did not know where our next meal would come from. It was rare, but it did happen. Other times we enjoyed life to the fullest. We've had our good times and bad times, but we chose to endure them together.

At times I became frustrated because my refrigerator was not full of the type of food I wanted to eat. The majority of the time there was only water or drinks in the fridge. That was because any time I bought meat or other perishable items; they would thaw out and spoil because of the lack of electricity. We usually had food, although it may have not been exactly what I wanted to eat. If I could have eaten the traditional Nigerian foods, I would have had no problem at all.

I did have some great friends who thought of me often. When they traveled to America and returned, they brought snacks for me: a pack of Doritos, M&M's or taco seasoning. It was a luxury even to have real butter, cheese, Ziploc bags, or a quality box of cereal. Some of my best memories are when we would be invited for dinner with some of my American missionary friends.

Food tended to be a big temptation in my life. I understood why Adam and Eve gave in and ate the fruit when they were tempted by the devil, even though they were told by God not to eat from a particular tree.

Early in my stay, I would cry when I went to bed at night and cry when I woke up in the morning. As soon as I got up, I would be so unhappy to know that I was still living in Nigeria. Culture shock got the best of me many times. I stayed inside my house day in and day out because I was more comfortable being in my home. The minute that I would go out, I would miss my American home even more and the reality of my life would sadden me. I also had to take care of the kids and the house. We only had one car and Albert needed the car to go to work and take care of business. For so long I felt miserable and thought that my life was the worst that anyone would ever have to go through. I later learned that there is always someone going through something far more difficult than I could imagine.

One day I saw a homeless man on Ahmadu Bello Way, carrying what seemed like thirty "Ghana Must Go" bags, lightweight nylon zippered bags. I wondered how he has able to tote all of those bags around. I wondered why he was carrying them, because he couldn't have had anything of importance in the bags. It became an example to me of the way many of us carry baggage around for years. In my mind, I told myself that it looked so ridiculous, and I would no longer carry any baggage in my life, allowing it to weigh me down.

If you are still carrying things in your past, let them go. If someone has hurt you and you're still holding on to that pain, let it go. Put those bags down and walk away. If you don't, it will just weigh you down and prevent you from being all that God wants you to be. Don't worry, God will carry those bags that you left behind and he will destroy them for you. You never have to think of them or look at them again.

These were the times that I had to cling to the word of God. It was easier with a church family and friends. Once we give our lives to Christ, we must do as God says in 2 Corinthians 6:14: "You are not the same as those who do not believe. So do not join yourselves to them. Good and bad do not belong together. Light and darkness cannot share together." I had to make sure that I did not allow influences from unbelievers tempt me to do things that would dishonor God during the hard times.

I was blessed to be surrounded by so many missionaries. However, I rarely shared my struggles with anyone because I knew that everyone had their own problems to deal with. If anyone would ask me how I was doing, I would just say "I am doing well, how are you?"

Missionaries go to share the Word of God. I went there and gave my life to Christ and was influenced greatly by the missionaries. I had never met a missionary until I went to Nigeria. God sent me there for a reason! People used to ask me, "What mission are you with?" and I would answer, "I am not with any mission." It didn't take long to realize that my mission was my family.

After many years, I realized what God was trying to do in my life. I truly believe that everything happened for a reason. God puts us in places and situations that at the time we may question, but He knows best. We may not be able to see what He is doing for us at the time; but if we allow God to take control of our lives, we will later be able to see His good works.

As each year would come and go, the missionaries would go home to visit their families, while I felt like I was the only white person being left behind. They would ask me, "Are you going home this year?"

I would let them know that I wouldn't be going home, trying hard not to let the pain I was feeling show on my face.

People would ask me, "How is your family back home? Are you speaking to them?"

I replied by saying, "Yeah, yeah, they are doing fine. I talk to them!"

All along I wanted someone to know how I felt inside, that none of my family members once called me to see how I was doing. I was the one that always had to call and speak to them to see how they were doing. If I called my brother, he never once asked me how my children were getting along, or how my husband was doing, or even how I was faring.

I began to love Nigeria even more during those times, simply because Nigerians always greet each other asking "How are you? How is your family? How is work? How are the kids?" and on and on.

Sometimes it could be annoying to stand there and keep saying "Fine, fine, fine, fine" over and over again. I later understood that it is important because in Nigeria basically all we have is each other as we struggle through our daily lives together trying to survive.

For some time, I was angry with my husband because I felt like it was his fault that I was in such a predicament. I finally understood that the past didn't matter anymore. What really matters is what lies ahead. I had a choice to either waste my time and energy being upset, or take full advantage of the life God gave me. I began to live out the verse I read in Ephesians 5:16: "Use every chance you have for doing good, because these are evil times."

I also began to understand what it's like for a man who has the responsibility of taking care of a family in Nigeria, or any other country for that matter. I learned that if I stressed him out, then Albert couldn't focus on his role to be a father and a husband. I had to accept him for who he was and be grateful for what he provided. After all, he would give me anything within his power. Albert was (and is) a loving and faithful husband and father.

The Lord and Nigeria taught me to be content in my life, but I was hardheaded and it took me several years to come around to that idea. When I saw others suffering around me, it touched my heart. I was surrounded by poverty, and the people around me needed help. I could no longer feel sorry for myself, especially when I saw how people around me were suffering just to get food or water for that day. I could no longer complain about having to take a bath using a bucket or to get my water from a well. I saw people walking long distances to get just one bucket of water for their house or old women carrying firewood on their heads. I no longer felt sorry for myself like I did for in the first few years in Nigeria. God opened my eyes and showed me just how precious life is. He showed me how blessed I really was, when all along I thought I was suffering. I was able to give help to those in need. Giving to those who could not help themselves gave me a new sense of fulfillment and purpose in life.

By crying and being ungrateful for so long, I felt I had disappointed God. I came from a country full of riches. Growing up in America makes many of us spoiled and ungrateful. God wanted me just to be content with what He had given me. And so did my husband, he wanted me just to be appreciative of his efforts.

First Timothy 6:6 says "A godly life brings huge profits to people who are content with what they have." The moment I accepted this verse and became content in my life is when things began to change for me. I had wasted a lot of valuable time being unhappy—time I could have used to accomplish so much.

I cannot say I've never had another challenging time when I missed home and wanted to go back or was tired of the life in Nigeria, but I allowed God to comfort me through His Word. I had to learn to accept my circumstances as they were, and to look at the things that I did have instead of wishing for things that I did not have. I stopped feeling sorry for myself and gave God full authority in my life.

Being grateful for the green grass in the rainy season, the bed I slept in every night, the house that was given to us (we never once had to pay rent), the fresh air, my beautiful children and—most especially—good health, these were choices I made. I sang, "Count your blessings, name them one by one." Drowning in self-pity had kept me from seeing the good in my life. That selfishness made me a prisoner in my own body.

When I compared my life with others, I didn't realize I was hurting myself. I felt pity and wondered, why me? I learned I could not stand by watching while others lived their lives; because if I did, I stopped living my own life. I didn't want to wake up and see I had wasted valuable years. I found I could never move forward in life or be content if I looked at what other people own or what they have done. Material things would no longer make me who I am and I will not be remembered for the things I own or the amount of money I have. People will remember me for how I treated others, how I raised our children, and by my accomplishments. I have value because I am a daughter of God.

One time while relaxing in my living room, I could hear crying and wailing. I wondered what happened. I stuck my head out the gate, curious to see what was going on. It was normal for someone to be passing by my gate anytime that I stepped out. As a little boy passed by I asked him, "What happened?"

He replied, "Somebody died!"

I soon learned to recognize the sound of a cry which meant somebody had died in the neighborhood. It was a sound I heard often, and I wasn't sure if I was noticing it more because I was more aware or if death was happening more. The more it happened, the more I realized how quickly we can be here one day and gone the next.

Strangers often knocked at my gate because they knew a white woman lived inside the compound. I never refused what they were asking. I was blessed to be able to help someone in need. It was a bit frustrating at times, but I knew what Jesus would have done if He was the one who answered the gate. How could I say no to someone who was begging me for food to feed their children? After all, what I have belongs to Him; everything that I have today is because of God. I could easily be in the position of that person.

Proverbs 28:27 "Whoever gives to the poor will have everything he needs, but the one who ignores the poor will receive many curses.

I began to understand that America is not heaven. I asked myself, *How long will I continue to be so ungrateful because I have to eat rice every day? How could I be so selfish when there are people who live right next to me who only eat once a day?* Some people don't even have the privilege of eating once a day. God showed me that the most important thing in this life is to know where we will go when we die. I could no longer spend countless hours and days worrying about going back to America, especially since I had no idea when that time would come. I chose to make the most of my circumstance instead of wasting away years of my life in pain. I allowed God to comfort me.

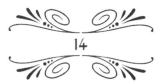

14

In 2008, I was asked to fill a temporary position at the missionary school, Hillcrest. For six months I filled in for the librarian, who had served for two years and was going back to America. The new librarian had not come yet from the United States. I felt honored to have the experience of working in a missionary school. I had been staying at home, but needed to get out of the house after awhile, so Grace stayed home with my son while I went to work at Hillcrest.

I felt sad that I did not get to finish my education before moving to Nigeria, and I wondered when I would be able to complete my studies. At times I wondered if I was just going to become dumber by living there!

A lady came to visit Nigeria after her boyfriend passed away. When I met her, she told me she was taking classes through the University of Phoenix. That gave me an idea of how I could continue with my own education. I contacted a few universities and chose University of Phoenix to pursue a degree in Elementary Education. I started my first class in November of 2008. I thought, *Finally, I can work toward something and better myself!*

The first year of studying was the most difficult for me. At that time, it was not possible to get wireless Internet in the house, so I had to go to an Internet café. I had to pay hourly for the Internet service, and funds were not always available. Thankfully, Albert started doing some work at the Internet café inside our church compound. I was then able to use the café anytime I needed to as partial payment for his services. Albert worked there just so I could have a secure place to continue my studies. He also wanted me to succeed.

I persisted through the inconsistency of the electricity and Internet connections. Many times it would take 10 or 15 minutes to load one page. When it would finally load, the electricity would go off. Then I had to wait for the generator to come on, for the computers to start up again, and for the Internet to reboot. I felt like giving up many times, but I knew this was the only way for me to get my education while keeping my family together. I continued like that for about a year until Multilinks (an Internet provider) made it possible to get a wireless modem in our house.

After that, the battery for my laptop stopped working so when the power went off, it shut off immediately. I constantly clicked the save button to make sure I didn't lose any of my work. We bought a battery online in America and had it sent to someone to bring to Nigeria when they came. For some reason it didn't work, so we figured we bought a bad battery. We bought a second one, which also did not work. Even though it was the most frustrating thing to me, I never gave up because I knew I was working toward something I had wanted for a long time. I was not going to let anything get in the way that would cause me to fail! Eventually I bought a new laptop.

I gave praise to our God when I completed my Associate Degree in June of 2011. Then I decided to change my field so I would be able to work with children who have been abused and neglected. I completed my BA in Human Service in September of 2013.

We could have filed for Albert's green card several years ago, but I wanted to finish my degree so I could get a good job when we moved back to America. I was given a second chance to complete my education and a chance to nurture, love, and teach my children. God opened my eyes to a wealth of knowledge. Only God, the one that forgives us of all of our sins, our shortcomings, and our mistakes could do this for me. I took advantage of the abundance of time on my hands to study and learn as much as I could. God had given me a second chance. It would have been more difficult to complete my studies in America, because I would have had to work many hours away from my kids. It would have been more difficult to study and write papers each week. Plus, my mindset needed to be changed in order for me to grow.

We also had no idea what to expect from Immigration since we thought Albert was banned from returning to the United States for ten years and I would have to prove extreme hardship. Imagine— the person who couldn't deal with living in Nigeria now wanted to stay a little bit longer! I came to love Nigeria, and her people became my family. For a long time I was blind to the opportunities before me; but when I let my guard down, my life changed.

Before I went to Nigeria I never really experienced the presence of

God in my life. I never truly knew what I wanted to do with my life or what my purpose was on this earth. Each one of us has a purpose and we cannot know what that purpose is until we accept Jesus Christ into our lives and allow Him to take over.

Before coming to Nigeria I had given my life to Christ many times, but my life never changed because I did not really allow God to take control. Once I finally gave Him that control, He left me with a wonderful story to tell the world.

I had to allow God to guide me on this path and to put my trust and faith in Him for what He wanted to do in my life. Sometimes we have to make certain decisions in life, even if it makes us uncomfortable. In the long run, we will not regret the decision that we made. When placed in an uncomfortable situation it is human nature to search for any possible way out. But I truly believe God placed me in this situation so He could allow me to have an abundant life. Second Corinthians 5:17 says, "Therefore, if anyone is in Christ, the new creation has come: The old has gone, the new is here!" That is how we begin to rise above our circumstances! Of course, it cannot happen all in one day. The Lord changes us one step at a time.

I do not believe God causes us to suffer. Many times when I thought I was suffering, it was all a matter of perspective. I allowed the devil to make me think my life was horrible and that I would never amount to anything. However, I can overcome Satan's whispers in my ear if I study the Word of God. Those words are my tools to fight the devil's lies when he tells me, "You are weak, stupid, and helpless." When I gave God full authority in my life and He began working in me, Satan began to attack my mind; but I was able to resist him through God's Word.

15

In 2009, after living in Nigeria for three years, I traveled to America with our children to see my extended family members. It was difficult for me to leave my husband for two months and it was difficult for him to see his entire family leave him behind. I watched Albert cry because he was afraid I might not come back to be with him. Perhaps he feared he would never see his children again, or maybe he was just dreading the loneliness. Some of our friends wondered if I would come back, while others had faith that I would. However, my experiences in that trip only rejuvenated my enthusiasm to go back to Nigeria.

When we arrived at the airport in New York, before we caught our flight to Atlanta, I rushed over to McDonald's. I couldn't wait to eat those favorite foods. Whitney and I were very excited; but Micah, who was two years old, looked at the hamburger and said, "What's this?"

"It's a hamburger, Micah."

He refused to eat it, so I was happy to eat an extra one. I felt like I could eat several! I was finally feeling the comfort of being in my own culture with my own food. I gave Micah some French fries and he ate those since he was used to eating "chips." My son loved Nigerian food and had a hard time eating American food, so the tables were turned. Micah loved to eat egusi soup with pounded yam and lots of pomo (cow's skin) with his daddy. He also loved to eat rice, since that's what we ate the majority of the time. I had to make sure I always had some rice for him to eat. But much of the time he refused to eat anything and I began to worry about him. My little boy had never been to America and he was now experiencing his own culture shock.

When my sister-in-law met us at the airport in Atlanta, she bought Teddy Grahams and apple juice for us. I cannot find the words to express how it felt to finally be home and eat cookies that were of good quality! As we got into her car and drove home, I sat in the back seat and enjoyed the ride: smooth roads, working traffic lights, cleanliness, fresh air, and a car that had not been spoiled by years of dust that could deteriorate the seats and the carpet. I could imagine what it would be like for someone visiting America for the first time. Somehow, even though I grew up in America and didn't go to Nigeria until I was 26, I was amazed at seeing such a rich country.

I had heard all about the recession in America and how so many people had lost their jobs and the economy was down; but after being in Nigeria for three years, I couldn't help but see America as the same great country I had left. The problems from the recession were not visible. Americans still had many luxuries that people in developing countries don't have.

In those three years of living in Nigeria, I had seen so much that I had a different view of life. As I returned to my home country, I cried on the plane as I thought of the children who lived near my house in Nigeria. I often gave them biscuits (cookies), "puff puff" (donuts), or my children's outgrown clothes. That may not sound like much to an American, but it meant a lot to those children.

While we were in America, Micah needed to get a visa since he did not have his Nigerian passport yet. I didn't have to apply for one myself since I had a multiple entry visa just for being married to a Nigerian. As I walked down the street in Atlanta on my way to the Nigerian Embassy, several Nigerians talked to me when they saw me backing Micah. I had been carrying Micah like that from the time he was born. These people realized I had a close connection to their country.

It is interesting to compare the two countries: one that had reached its highest peak and another that had gained independence only 50 years previously. Yet Nigeria seemed to be a superior country when it came to relationships. The people care so much for each other and go out of their way to show it. They share what little they have and smile even though they lack food, water, power, and education for their children. Nigerians make a special effort to show compassion and care for others.

America looked so beautiful to me as I saw it with new eyes. You never know how good something is until it is taken from you. When I was living there, I didn't know the rest of the world looked at my country in awe and that many people yearned to immigrate. I never knew what it really meant to be an American, even though I learned to sing "I am proud to be an American where at least I know I am free." I never took the time to think about where we got our water, which came rushing freely out of the tap, never stops, and is always clean. I never knew how blessed we were to have electricity every day of our lives.

It used to frustrate me that the law made us wear seat belts and buckle our children into car seats; that is, until I went to Nigeria and saw small babies standing in the front seat. I finally realized that the laws were for our own protection. If we don't obey the law, we will pay a fine. This is just the beginning of the differences of the governments in America and Nigeria. Many Americans complain about what our government is or is not doing; but one cannot see the greatness of America until they have lived in or visited a less fortunate nation.

I called my father to tell him I was in Fayetteville, Arkansas, a three-hour drive from him. I thought God had finally answered my prayers, because my father finally wanted to come and see me and my children! He came to visit us with my brother and Grandma. They stayed for just a few hours, but it meant the world to me that my father had driven three hours just to see me. It felt so good to see all of them at once after so many years of being apart.

As I drove back to Atlanta where my sister-in-law lived, 11 hours away, my Aunt Jean called to say that my father wanted me to come to his house. This was another answer to prayer since my father never wanted me to bring my children to his house. Unfortunately, I had already passed his house en route to Atlanta. I wished so badly that I hadn't missed the opportunity to sit in my father's house with my children.

Today, I have yet to receive a phone call from my father. He still has no relationship me, my children, or my husband.

When I returned to Nigeria, the process of getting through Immigration and Customs was a smooth experience once again. When they saw that my last name was Owonubi, they let me pass through without even checking my bags. One woman looked at me and said, "Iya, you married a Nigerian!"

The "touts" that worked in the airport helped me carry my luggage to the car. Albert tipped him and I gave him the juice and cookies that I had gotten from the plane. I knew he would enjoy them. After living in Nigeria, you learn to keep everything, because somebody will eat it or use it.

Albert, the children and I were all so happy to be reunited! Everyone

I saw told me how nice I looked. I felt refreshed, and evidently it showed. I was able to get a fresh haircut and get my hair dyed to cover the grey. I also bought new clothes for the children and me.

Everybody I saw greeted me warmly, welcomed me back to Nigeria, and then asked what I brought for them. It was overwhelming because I felt it wasn't possible for me to bring a gift for everyone, especially since my husband comes from a big family and our church has many members. I brought back about 15 pounds of chocolate to share with the many people that would come around expecting something.

For myself, I bought about 30 boxes of macaroni and cheese. To save room in packing, I only took the sauce packets. I could buy macaroni in Nigeria!

16

After settling back into regular life, I realized I needed to do something productive. Since I only went out of the house about once a month to buy food and went to church on Sundays, I had time on my hands. A close friend needed help with her four-year-old daughter while she worked. She wanted to send her to Hillcrest School, but they don't accept students until they turn five.

This seemed like a good time for me to start a preschool. Teaching children was a good option for me—my son was preschool age, and I had finished my degree in Elementary Education. The house next door was owned by the Owonubi family and it would be an ideal location for the preschool. I was not ready to put Micah in a Nigerian school, and I wanted to teach him myself anyway. Teaching Micah was a great privilege, I didn't have that opportunity with Whitney.

We started the school with just Micah and my friend's little girl; but people soon heard what I was doing, we ended up with twelve children as students. It was an International school because the children were from America, Nigeria, United Kingdom, Australia, India, Germany, and Lebanon. People came to trust me with their children and were happy with the results.

One day God placed a very special little girl in my life. I will call her Mary. I learned that she was not going to school because her family could not afford the fees. Mary's father died in the village and her mother had remarried. Some women who remarry in Nigeria disown their children because the new husband does not want to care for any children from a previous marriage. Mary lived with extended family members who were Muslims. When I opened my school I told her, "Come to school on Monday and dress up in your best clothes!" She had never been to school. She said she was nine years old, but she kept saying that for several years. She did not know her actual age and had never celebrated a birthday.

The first day she attended school, she didn't have any lunch, even though I told her to bring one. "Where is your lunch?" I asked. She just looked up at me, not knowing what to say. I said, "Run home and get something that you can eat!"

"There is no food!" she said while hanging her head.

From that moment on, I decided that I would include her when making lunches for my children to take to school. Sometimes she would come to school without having eaten breakfast; she appeared to not have any energy. The mother in the home where Mary lived said if she gave her food, she would sleep and not be able to learn. So she didn't feed Mary. I tried to explain to her guardian that she needed food to be able to concentrate, and that breakfast is considered the most important meal of the day. They never once sent food with her to school, though they did send cloudy, dirty water in a plastic coke bottle a few times. Many times Mary would come in the morning and lie down because she was so weak from hunger.

I gave her some of Whitney's outgrown clothes to replace her own worn and stained clothing, but her guardian wouldn't allow her to wear them. I was told that she gave them to her own children.

Sometimes Mary would come to school without taking a bath because she couldn't get hot water for her bath. I would go home and heat water so she could bathe. It brought me such great joy to see the big smile on her face simply because she was able to take a hot bath. Apparently she had to take cold baths at home because of the lack of power and because nobody cared enough to help her.

Mary came to our school every day for nearly two years. Her extended family never asked her how she was doing with her studies. In fact, they were jealous because she was receiving a free education and some of their many biological children were not. Some of their children were attending school, but it was difficult for them to pay the fees.

Eventually I decided to close the preschool. There were many reasons for this, but the main one was to give me time to start filing for my husband's green card. I told Mary I was going to put her into a school nearby since she had learned her alphabet and numbers. At the very least she would be able to count money and to read. If nothing else, she would now have a voice. Before I could put her into school, her family placed her into a public government school, which they could have done in the beginning. I was just grateful that my involvement gave her a better chance in life.

I received strength by knowing I could help others who couldn't possibly repay me. Luke 14:14 says, "Then you will be blessed because they have nothing and cannot pay you back. But you will be repaid when the good people rise from the dead."

For the first five years I lived in Jos, there was a man who lived at the end of my street. He was known in the community as "Waldo" or "Wally," because he slept outside a wall surrounding a missionary compound. He wore the same clothes everyday and he covered himself with a small plastic tarp during the rainy season. He frequently passed my house with his bare feet and dreadlocks, never allowing anyone to look him in the eye. He often dug in the trash for food and smoked "Indian hemp" (marijuana). I tried to give him money or food, just as many others did; but he shouted at me, "I do not want your money."

One day a missionary managed to reach out to him through a cup of tea, by the grace of God! The missionary took him to a nearby rehab to get help. There his life changed and he later shared his testimony. God truly protected this man from sickness since he slept outside for so many years. I had malaria many times, and I was not sleeping outside with the mosquitoes like this man was. I often thought it was cruel that thousands of people must have passed him while he lived in the street like an animal. In reality, many people actually tried to help him but he rejected their help. How can we see another human being living in such a state and continue to go on with our lives?

Every time I saw this man on the roadside, it helped me to be grateful for what I had in my life: a roof over my head, a nice cozy bed to sleep in, and food to eat. I began to thank God every night when I lay down in my bed to sleep. I remembered this passage when I became weary or worried about finances:

Matthew 6:25-34 Therefore I tell you do not worry about your life, what you will eat or drink; or about your body, what you will wear. Is not life more than food and the body more than clothes? Look at the birds of the air; they do not sow or reap or store away in barns, and yet your heavenly Father feeds them. Are you not much more valuable than they? Can any one of you by worrying add a single hour to your life? And why do you worry about clothes? See how the flowers of the field grow. They do not labor or spin. Yet I tell you that not even Solomon in his entire splendor was dressed like one of these. If that is how God clothes the grass of the field, which is here today and tomorrow is thrown into the fire, will he not much more clothe you—you of little faith? So do not worry, saying, 'What shall we eat?' or 'What shall we drink?' or 'What shall we wear?' For the pagans run after all these things, and your heavenly Father knows that you need them.   But seek first his kingdom and his righteousness, and all these things will be given to you as well. Therefore do not worry about tomorrow, for tomorrow will worry about itself. Each day has enough trouble of its own.

During my first few years in Nigeria, Christmas was a difficult time for me. I missed the way I had always celebrated Christmas in America. I spent my time making American food to comfort myself. But when people came to our house for the traditional Christmas Day visit, they didn't want to eat American food; so I stopped making it. I realized that I was in Nigeria, so I needed to make food for Nigerians if I wanted to have any visitors that day.

Each year, we would buy about ten chickens and cook oodles of rice and chin-chin (bite-size cookies) outside on a fire, and have many soft drinks available. It was easier to cook that many chickens outside on the wood fire with a much bigger pot than I could have used in my kitchen. I often called the children from the neighborhood to eat. I never let food go to waste in my house after knowing that I could easily call somebody to eat it. The children were more excited to be inside our compound than to have rice since most people have plenty of rice in their house on Christmas Day. They were more interested in eating the meat, since it is too expensive for most of them to eat meat very often.

We spent the first three years without a Christmas tree, which is abnormal for an American family. There are many children in Nigerian who have never had a Christmas tree. Their only gift is usually a new outfit of clothes. God always provided for us on that day. My friend Mary Beth sent her husband around to share gifts with us, and we would get things from family members in America sometimes. It was never easy to do Christmas shopping for our children in Jos because there was a lack of quality things and other items were overpriced. Even though I was bothered by the fact that my children didn't have a Christmas tree, I knew they would have no ill effects. They would know Jesus Christ, and they would grow up in a loving home with both of their parents. That was far more important than a Christmas tree!

17

In November of 2008, I was still working at Hillcrest School. I woke up one morning, got ready, and prepared to drop Whitney off at school on the way to work. I discovered that her school was closed. I wondered why they hadn't given us any notice, so I drove on to work. People were standing at the entrance and no one was allowed to pass through the gate. One man who lived inside the compound looked at me and said, "Go back home and stay inside!" I looked at him in complete confusion and asked, "Why? What's happening?"

He said, "There is fighting in town!" Without asking more questions, I rushed home to tell Albert the news. He said it was Muslims and Christians fighting one another. I never really had much interest in politics, but people said it was a political/religious fight. I still did not understand why they were fighting. I later found out "fighting" actually meant some people were being slaughtered in their own homes! We heard that many houses and cars had been burned, people were killed, and shops had been destroyed in the market. We all stayed in the house for fear of what was happening—this was not some movie, but real life. We could see a big cloud of black smoke coming from the other side of the town and we could hear gunshots. By the next morning, things had gotten worse and the violence had reached our side of the town in GRA/Tudun Wada (Government Reserved Area). I stepped outside our gate to see what was happening. The youths in the area were outside, ready to fight in the battle. They were ready to kill any Muslim who came across their path because many Christians had been killed. The youths were tramping through the neighborhood holding makeshift weapons they found lying around their houses, such as chains and bars. A young boy had a chain wrapped around his hand ready to fight, while we heard that the Muslims had machetes ready to cut off Christians' heads.

The youths paced furiously and destroyed the tables across the road from our house. Those tables were used by a woman to market her tomatoes and other vegetables. At that time, we thought the youths were the trouble makers. Later we realized that they actually protected our neighborhood. They were able to force out the Muslims from our area and keep us all safe from surprise attack. The Christian youths stopped cars and demanded that the driver and passengers quote John 3:16 or the Lord's Prayer. I worried about the Christians who could not quote that verse or passage.

We decided it was best to go inside the house and lock the doors. Then Albert and I became curious when we heard a commotion outside. We poked our heads outside the gate to see a car which had been set on fire at the intersection near our house. I never knew if anyone was in the car when it burned. I just could not believe that I was surrounded by such violence. I had never experienced anything like that in America!

Surprisingly, I was not afraid of what was happening around me. Since giving my life to Christ and growing in His Word, I felt a sense of peace that God was going to protect my family. I always felt as if God had His angels surrounding our compound. We seldom had a guard at our gate and we didn't lock the gate much of the time because of the many tenants living in the compound. I hid beside the road while I took a picture of the car being burned in the middle of the road. I felt like I was an international reporter. It was all so foreign to me.

After standing outside the gate for some time, we heard a crowd of people next to our house scream, "Jeeeeesus!" We looked across the street and saw an old Muslim man lying on the ground in a puddle of his own blood. The youth who struck him across his head with a chrome bar had already left the scene for fear of what would happen next. A few of us rushed to check on the bleeding man. Albert went to get the car from our house, which was directly across the street from the incident. He helped the man stand up, get in the backseat of the car; then rushed to the nearest hospital, which was less than a mile away. He left the man there and hurried back home.

While Albert was attempting to put this man in the car, those surrounding us asked, "Do you know him?"

Albert replied, "No!" I suppose they were curious why Albert would help a Muslim man when our fellow Christians were being killed, but that didn't matter to Albert. There was no way he could walk away from the man and leave him to die in his own blood.

I saw a soldier walking down the road just after the incident. I looked at him and said, "There was a man who almost died, did you see him?" I was trying to report the incident. A woman behind him heard me talking and waved her hands and shook her head, "No!"

It flustered me but I followed her advice and went home. Once I got there, I realized she was protecting our family and the neighborhood. I didn't know if he was a Muslim or Christian, and reporting the incident would have been like putting gas on a fire that was already out of control. At the time, I had no idea that I could have made the situation worse. I was thinking like an American, that we could trust and get help from any nearby official when needed.

That night I did not sleep at all. Besides the gunshots throughout the night, many thoughts plagued my mind. I wondered if that man survived and if the doctors were able to stop the bleeding soon enough. I later found out that Plateau Hospital had many other casualties. I wondered about his family and knew they must be worried that he did not make it home. I prayed that God would save him and keep him alive.

The day after the incident, Albert decided it was best for us to leave our house and stay in Abuja with his brother-in-law until the violence ended. We were afraid of what could happen to us since he had helped a Muslim man. We were told that, after we left, the Christian youths threatened to burn down the house next door to us. Christians lived upstairs and a Muslim family lived downstairs. The Christians pleaded with the youths not to burn the house down because it would affect the Christians upstairs.

We stayed in Abuja for a few days until I insisted we go back because I couldn't tolerate the heat in Abuja. I didn't care what was happening in the town anymore. I just wanted to be in my house. Shortly after we arrived back home, the government ordered a 24-hour curfew in the city of Jos. Luckily, I always kept certain foods stocked up, or we would have been without food for three full days. The small shop next to our house did open briefly to sell to people in the neighborhood. It was a good thing, since the neighboring houses could not afford to keep food in bulk. Nearby soldiers shouted at people to hurry and get back inside their houses. As I snuck out of the house in an attempt to get any food I could, a soldier holding his gun looked at me and said, "Oyibo, where you de go now?"

I replied politely to keep peace, "I just want to buy something from the shop really fast, sir."

He shouted, "Hurry up!" I rushed to buy what I could and ran back into the house. A neighbor lady knocked at our gate and begged, "Please, give me food for my children, they are hungry and I have no food to give them." I was more than happy to give her food for her children and was grateful to God that He made it possible for me to be in a position to share. I put some rice, yam, and spaghetti in a bag and told Grace to give it to the lady.

I watched from the gate and saw her kneel down and say, "Nagode, Allah!" which means "Thank you God!" It always brought me great joy to give to others in need.

Finally the fighting stopped and the curfew was lifted. We were so happy to be back at work and to be able to get out of the house after being forced to stay inside for several days. We drove around town to see the aftermath of the violence and were amazed by the amount of destruction throughout the town. The government had deployed soldiers around the entire town to ensure safety. Sadly, that wasn't the end of the fighting; the turmoil between Christians and Muslims has continued.

We were blessed to have many ministers in our church because Evangel Theological Seminary was located in the same compound as the church. It was extremely sad when we found out that one of the pastors had been slaughtered during the crisis. They found his body with many parts missing. After being hacked into pieces, his body was burned. The pastor left behind his wife and children, who continued to be members of the church after his death. Every time I saw one of his children in the church, I couldn't help but think of their father who was killed because of his faith. It must have been terribly painful to endure. I couldn't believe what was happening right before my eyes, but each experience opened my eyes even more to situations around the world.

Christians were told not to buy beef or apples from the Muslims because they were poisoned. Nobody knew whether it was true, but no one wanted to take the chance of being killed. Many people avoided buying those items for a time.

A few months later I went to the shop across the street from our house and saw a Muslim man with a big scar on the back of his head. As I looked more closely at the man's head, the shop owner noticed and said, "That's him." He was the man my husband helped after he was attacked by the Christian youth. The shop owner told the man who I was (in Hausa, since he didn't understand English) while they both looked at me. The Muslim man kept saying, "Nagode!" which means "Thank you!" I was so happy to see he had survived and was well.

One Saturday evening Albert needed to do some work in the church, so I dropped him off and went into town to buy a few things. I parked and crossed the street to buy yams near Challenge Bookshop. When I was ready to cross back to the car, I realized the traffic was so heavy I could barely make it back across the street. The nearby shop owners began locking their shops and the cars all seemed to be going away from town. I asked someone nearby what was happening and they told me there was fighting in town. I thought, *Oh, Jesus, not again! Not now! Not here!*

I was parked on the corner, which made it nearly impossible for me to get out because of traffic and people running helter-skelter. This time I was not in my home; I was alone and I was afraid. Thankfully, I was no longer a "Learner" at driving in Nigeria and was able to make my way out, despite the fact that one lane of the road was made into four with cars scrambling to get out of the area. I made it safely back to the church to pick up Albert.

In 2010 a nearby village was attacked in the middle of the night. The attackers fired gunshots and burned the roofs of the houses to make everyone run outside so they could attack them. They killed nearly every woman and child in the entire village. A friend of ours visited the village and took pictures. The photos were one of the saddest and most inhumane sights I have ever seen. One specific picture haunts me to this day: two little girls were apparently sleeping on a mat on the floor. They did not have the luxury of a mattress. Their bodies lay beside their heads, which had been hacked in half by a machete. I felt such sorrow for the families who had survived in this village.

Amazingly, I did not live in fear while being so close to such evil brutality. I allowed God to open my eyes to the realities of how the world had become so wicked. I realized we cannot live one day on this earth without depending on God for His guidance and protection. I became more and more convinced that our only shield in life is Jesus Christ, and we must cling to Him as we try to raise our children in a cruel world. If we do not teach our children the Word of God, they will become a part of the world. We heard stories of fake soldiers, men who posed as soldiers in an attempt to kill Christians. Everyone I began to realize that the military could not be trusted, and the only real protection was in our Lord Jesus Christ.

On Christmas Eve that year we experienced our first bomb blast in Jos. It was the beginning of a series of bomb blasts throughout the country. The bombing just before Christmas was an attempt to destroy the celebration of Jesus' birth, and was an attack on the religion and beliefs of Christianity.

That Christmas was a lonely one with no movement around the entire town for fear of what could happen. Christmas was usually a time spent visiting others throughout the day, eating fried rice, chin-chin, and meat. As a result of the bombings, people stopped moving around that Christmas Day. Instead they went to church and came back home. The actions of the Muslims only made the Christians draw closer to God, though their intention was to make us weak in our faith. Most of us began to thank God everyday that we were still alive, because hundreds of people lost their lives. We began to spend more time with God, thanking Him, praying for His protection over our lives, and clinging more to Him. Our lives were in His hands: if we died, we knew there was a place for us in Heaven.

On February 26, 2012, at 7 a.m. while the house was quiet, a loud sound woke me from my sleep. Startled and confused, I shook Albert asking him, "Did you just hear that?"

He said, "Yeah, I think it was thunder!"

Obviously, he wasn't awake yet. It wasn't usual to have thunder during the dry season when there was no rain. I thought there must have been a bomb because the sound shook the windows. I unlocked the front door and stepped outside our gate still believing it was a bomb. If that were the case, the people living in the slums outside our gate would also be outside trying to figure out what the noise was. Sure enough, all the neighbors had come out of their houses. They saw me stick my head out the gate and I asked, "What was that noise?"

Somebody replied, "Na bomb, COCIN Headquartas!" Her Pidgin English told me a bomb had gone off at COCIN Church Headquarters, which is just about a half mile from us.

I ran back into the house to tell Albert. We went next door to tell his sister-in-law and her husband. We learned that a suicide bomber had forced his car into the church compound. In the process, he ran over a woman and killed her. But, the suicide bomber did not die until the members of the church caught him and soldiers killed him.

Just a few weeks later, in the middle of church services, the pastor announced that St. Finbars' Catholic church in Rayfield had been bombed. That church was on the other side of town, close to

Whitney's school. We had a close friend who lived directly across from that church. When he came to visit, he showed us pictures of the damages to the church, of a woman who was killed whose arm was detached from her body, and a video of the suicide bombers being burned by the nearby crowd.

The town changed drastically after all the suicide bomb attacks. Every church placed barriers on the streets to prevent a bomber from forcing his car into the church building or the church compound. We could no longer park our cars inside the church property. Instead we parked on the street outside the compound. We could no longer carry a purse to church since a bag could possibly conceal a bomb. Security and police checkpoints were placed throughout the town. The checkpoints were especially thorough at the edges of town. They checked each individual or car that looked suspicious.

Two more bombs went off in the Tudun Wada area, which was our neighborhood. Thankfully, the bombs were much smaller than the ones that were placed in the churches. Albert's sister called from Lagos. "What is going on in your area? I hope you are okay!"

"We didn't hear anything, but we are safe and in the house!" Albert replied.

A few weeks before the bombs began going off, a letter was found in the neighborhood, very near our house. The letter was written from Boko Haram threatening to bomb our area in Tudun Wada. When we first heard about it and saw the note, we were skeptical. We did not want to believe that it was true; but when bomb blasts occurred just a few blocks from our house, we believed it.

18

By this time, almost seven years later, I decided it was time to start figuring out how to file for Albert's green card and see how the process worked since Jos was no longer a safe place to raise children. After all, we finally had a case of hardship to tell the Immigration Service.

I had contacted an immigration lawyer a few years back who was related to Albert. She told us that she would charge us $3,500 to take the case. That did not include all of the fees for the forms that needed to be filed with the United States Citizenship Immigration Service (USCIS). The total was nearly $7,500 for the entire process including paying the lawyer. We were overwhelmed, wondering how we would come up with that much money. In addition, the tickets for all of us to fly back to America would be around $8,000. Then we realized we no longer owned anything in America and had no place to go. We would also need money for a house and money for a car.

We started putting more trust and faith in God that He would make a way, when and if it was His will for us to go back to America. At one point, I felt like it would never happen. I used to wonder if I would spend the rest of my life in Nigeria. Getting everything we needed just seemed impossible, especially since none of my family members in America offered any help. They never asked, so I never told them about the situation.

After a while, I stopped depending on man, instead I put all my trust and faith in God. Proverbs 3:5 says, "Trust in the LORD with all your heart and lean not on your own understanding." God knows what we need before we even ask. He never gets tired of helping us. Luke 12:7 says, "But God even knows how many hairs you have on your head. Don't be afraid. You are worth much more than many sparrows." The same way God has watched over us during our entire time in Nigeria, He continued to prove His love for us as we continued to pray and put our faith in Him.

We sent $1,000 to the lawyer so that we could start the immigration process, not really knowing how we would pay the rest of the money. A few weeks later we received an email from the lawyer that we shouldn't worry about the remaining fee! After that, we were able to come up with the money for filing the first form. We waited until someone was leaving Nigeria to go to America, so they could mail that form to the lawyer. After she received it, she would look it over and file it for us.

One day I got a text from my friend Mary Beth that said, "Emma is going to the U.S. today, call him now!" Albert met him and gave him the documents to mail for us. Then it was waiting time: Emma's travel to the United States, mailing the form, the lawyer inspecting the form, and finally mailing it to USCIS. After that, we had to wait to hear from the USCIS. On April 13, 2012, we received an email from the USCIS informing us they had received the form and we should get a reply within five months. The process was finally in motion. God's time is the best time!

On May 26, 2012 we got a message from USCIS stating that they were sending out a letter requesting more information and evidence about our marriage. The letter would tell us what else we needed to provide, the deadline to submit it, and the address to which we should mail it. We just knew that God was in control because we had gotten the reply only a month after submitting the form. I became a bit worried about that letter making it to Nigeria, since the postal mail can be unreliable. I did not want us to miss the deadline, which would result in denial of the form. The lawyer assured me not to worry since our marriage is a bonafide marriage and that the form would be approved.

On June 11, 2012, Albert checked at the Post Office. The letter had arrived safe and sound! I couldn't wait for him to come home after work so that I could hold the letter in my hands. It was wonderful to hear from the USCIS. They had left a bitter taste in my mouth when they deported my husband. For several years I thought they didn't want to work in our favor. It felt good to be an American and that it was my right to have my husband come to my country with me! After reading the letter together, we looked at each other and smiled from ear to ear. We hugged each other. Albert knew how much it meant for me to go back to America and I wasn't going back without him.

The letter requested that Albert prove he had been in Nigeria for the past two years. After the deportation, he was banned for ten years; but since he was married to an American citizen, I could have filed for him after he had lived in Nigeria for only two years. We were shocked to learn that we only needed to wait two years instead of ten! How had we missed that important bit of information?

I looked at Albert and said, "It's okay, because I trust that it was God's will for us to be in Nigeria for this long. We needed to be here longer than those two years in order for God's plan for our lives to be complete!"

In the month of August, a friend was leaving Nigeria to go back to their country of Australia. He had an Internet modem that he had been using. Apparently, he paid for a year's worth at a time of Internet, but the subscription never stopped after that year. When he gave it to us, the Internet continued to work. We never had to pay for Internet again. I always saw these things as a part of God's hand in our lives, trying to help us along the way. We had struggled many times trying to pay for Internet while I continued to study online; but God relieved us from that worry while we were going through the lengthy and expensive process of getting Albert's green card and moving back to America.

We continued to gather the documents and send them to the lawyer. On August 10, 2012, I looked on the website and noticed that the form was approved—it had been approved in just four months. Once again we felt that God was in control, and we were ecstatic.

We waited for the next step towards getting Albert's green card. On September 7 we received an email from the National Visa Center (NVC) informing us that the petition had become eligible for further processing. Each time we heard from Immigration, we knew that we were one step closer. So I paid for the next form and again received confirmation from them.

It was now important to begin compiling information for our waiver packet where we had to prove extreme hardship to the USCIS. In the seven-page letter I informed them of what I faced when they deported my husband, along with all the other details. It took many months to compile proof and to make copies of all of the evidence. Since our lawyer lived in the US, it would be easier to process this paperwork. I wrote the letter and she approved of what I submitted; but she told me I needed to add more details. I gained a lot of knowledge on how to write and compile a waiver hardship packet. It felt great knowing that I had the ability to do this project. I pray

God will send someone my way that has gone through the same thing and has no idea how to begin so that I can help them.

One thing I couldn't tell the Immigration Department was that I actually found peace while living in Nigeria. I couldn't tell them how I thought that this was the best thing that probably happened for my life even through all of our hardships. I couldn't tell them that through this journey I was able to change my generation regardless of the hardships it took to accomplish it.

A friend that I went to school with in Bauxite agreed to help us in the sponsoring process for Albert. I had posted on Facebook how we needed a sponsor. I immediately told Albert about making the post; but he didn't like that I had done it, so I removed it right away. The post was probably on Facebook for 10 minutes; but it was just enough time that my high school friend saw it and offered to help. Although I am the sponsor, we needed a co-sponsor to cover the income requirements. It was necessary that we show proof of income to verify that Albert would not become dependent on public welfare. Having my friends co-sponsor Albert allowed me to continue to stay in Nigeria instead of having to leave my husband to seek employment in America and separate the family for a time. I mailed the documents to my friends in America and waited patiently. Within two weeks, they posted a picture of the letter on Facebook stating, "It's not every day you get mail from Nigeria!"

It was a relief that we were another step closer to what seemed like an impossible situation. On October 12, our friends sent us a message letting us know they were mailing the documents.

The next day we received an email informing us that the next form was available for processing. Within that email, it stated that the fee for that form was reduced on April 13, 2012. That was the same exact day that we started filing. The fee was reduced to nearly half of the previous amount. God never ceases to amaze me. The remaining money was just enough for Albert to renew his passport and get a security clearance from the police which is needed to file the next form. We sent in the next form and waited.

As we waited in hopes of getting an interview date, we received an email from the National Visa Center. Each time I saw an email from them, it was like sparks would go off inside my body. I couldn't wait to open the email and read what it said.

Unfortunately, this email from NVC said that we did not fill out one part of the form before we sent it. Within the form we were to detail every place that Albert had ever lived; and we had not completed the time that he was deported. We thought surely they would have known where he was during that time frame, but we needed to provide all the details for them. At any rate, they told us we needed to fill that part out and resend the form. We also needed to include any court documents from traffic tickets that he had received while in the U.S. Fortunately, as we began to gather those documents from the U.S., we were able to find someone to send a money order to the courts and request the records. It took nearly two months to get those documents to NVC. I thought, *Finally, Albert will get an interview date!*

Two weeks later we received another email, and I felt those sparks of excitement again. This time they were requesting that we send in a waiver named I-601A. The form was just released by the USCIS, and it was for those already living in the U.S. and living there illegally. It allows the filer the option of filing the form without having to be separated from their family. Since Albert was not living in the U.S., I knew they were giving us the wrong instructions; so I called NVC to notify them of the mistake. The lady I spoke with told me that it doesn't matter where Albert is living. I thought surely she doesn't know what she is talking about; so I hung up and called back again. This time the woman who answered said, "Oh, why are they doing this? Hold on while I see what to do!"

I waited on the line for a few minutes, and when she came back she told me, "You will to have to put it in writing; we can't handle this over the phone." I thought, *Oh goodness, not again!* We were so close, yet so far from success. I managed to get in contact with someone in the U.S. who helped me print the letter that I typed, which they sent to NVC by next-day delivery. Oh, I was thankful to get that letter to them that quickly. I still hoped to hear from them in a week or so with an interview appointment.

A few weeks passed and we still had not heard anything. I became worried and was impatient for the immigration process to be finished. I learned that I could request an expedited appointment date at the America Consulate in Lagos due to the insecurity of the living conditions in Jos. The National Visa Center had sent the request to the Consulate and was waiting for a reply. After a week, we received notification that the request for expediting the appointment date was denied. It was a bit discouraging, but it was better than the visa being denied. So again, we had to wait for the interview date.

By this time it had been almost a year since Albert had received any salary from the security company that was inherited from his parents after they died. It seemed to be the worst time for my husband to not get a salary. But I could clearly see the hand of God at work in our lives because we never lacked for anything. God always provided for us.

As Christmas approached, dealing with lack of funds was difficult; but God had done such a good work in me that I was able deal with what was happening without anxiety. There were times when Albert was worried because I was *not* stressed out because of the conditions. He would look at me to see if I was angry or upset only to find me in a peaceful state of mind. I knew and understood that our shortage of funds was just for a period of time and that it was not in my husband's control. Besides, this is normal for many Nigerians— sometimes they may have money and other times they may not. Everybody is just doing what they can do to earn money to survive. God also gave me understanding that we have to be patient and content with what we have. If we are not content and faithful with the little that we have, how can we ever expect him to give us more. One of the guards that lived in the compound next to us had not been paid for three months. I only learned of that situation when I heard he was coming home every day to eat guava off the tree because he was so hungry. I was more frustrated with the fact that he lived so close to me and was hungry and had not asked us for help. As soon as I heard about it, I did what I could to give him some food. Many times I was able to see clearly that, no matter how little we have, we can always give to others because there is often somebody much worse off than we are. Things may have not gone so well for us during that time, but at least we always had food and never went a day without it.

God was at work. Albert started getting jobs to build websites, to provide computers, to set up networks, and to do other jobs in that field, which was the work he wanted to do.

A Facebook friend posted that she was stressed out, trying to go to school and take care of her two children, and she was just 18 years old. Her two children have different fathers who do not help her at all. She lives in Benton, Arkansas, which is very close to where I grew up. I understood her plight, and I began to see how I could use my social work training. I wanted to reach out to help her. Since I had some cash in my U.S. checking account, I sent her a check for $30. This was someone I barely knew; she is a cousin of a friend. When I sent the check, I told her that I just wanted her to promise me that she will finish school.

A few days after that, I received an email from someone I had met on Facebook. She had heard a portion of my story from a Facebook page called "Mixed and Happy," about mixed-race marriages. The woman that owns the page requests that people send in their "Mixed and Happy" pictures to be displayed on her page. When I sent mine, I decided to add a short story of the racial part of my life. She posted the picture of me "backing" Micah along with the story. By the time I woke up the next morning, there was an email from her that my story had received more likes and comments than any other entry on her page. My story had nearly 3,000 likes and hundreds of shares and comments. From there, I received over 600 friend requests. A cousin of Albert's in Lagos wrote saying he sent my story to Linda Ikeji, a popular blogger. She liked my story, posted it on her blog, and from there my story could be found on many others sites and blogs. Others called to tell me that they heard about my story on the radio.

The email I received from the woman I met on Facebook said, "Crystal, I want to send your children clothes from America!" I was touched because I knew it was the hand of God once again. She sent us gift cards for when we come to the U.S. so that we can buy clothes for the children. The amount of the gift cards was $300. I had given $30 to someone who needed a boost, and God gave it back to me in the amount of $300.

This lady and I connected on Facebook to chat and she took pictures in the grocery store to show me. She asked me what foods I missed. As I told her of various foods, she took pictures of them and sent them to me. It actually made me miss home so much more and it got to a point where I would rather not have seen the pictures. As she was leaving the store, she took a picture of the cashier whom she had told of my story. The cashier was amazed. I asked my friend, "How did you speak to her because you said that you are deaf?" Immediately, she sent me a recorded message. As I listened to the message of her speaking, she said "Hi Crystal, how are you? I can't wait for you to come back home so that I can meet you! I love you! I can speak very well for a deaf person, right?" Tears instantly flowed from my eyes. I covered my face, and my body shook as I cried. I was so touched. It was like God was saying, "Crystal, if I want to reach you, I can reach you even through a person who is deaf!"

On the same day that I received her email, I also heard from another woman I had never met before. She is married to the brother of my husband's good friend. We shared something in common—we were both married to Nigerians. She had visited Nigeria, but said that she could never live there. She wanted my children's shoe sizes because she wanted to send shoes through her mother-in-law who was visiting in America and would be returning to Nigeria soon. Once again, I was thrilled of how God was working in my life. Micah just happened to need shoes for church and Whitney had told me that her school shoes were too small and she needed new ones. We were trying to save money for our transitioning back to the U.S. and didn't want to buy things in Nigeria that we would most likely not carry with us when we left. This friend sent the exact shoes that Whitney needed for school and church shoes for Micah without me ever telling her what they needed. I thought how God has a sense of humor. That was proof that he knows exactly what we need. I had never experienced such a thing in my entire life. I was receiving blessings from people I had never met, and I had never even asked for those things.

A few weeks after that, a cousin of my husband called said, "Hey, It's been a long time; I just wanted to greet you and see how your book is coming along!"

"Well, I am still working on it. Actually somebody is doing some editing at this moment. How are your wife and the children doing?"

"They are all doing fine!" he said.

Then the conversation ended, we said goodbye and I hung up the phone. Almost instantly he called right back. I thought it was weird and wondered what else he wanted to tell me.

"Do you remember the time when we spoke about your wanting to help others by possibly having your own organization?"

"Yeah, I remember, why?" I said.

"Please just send me your bank account number so I can wire some money."

"But why? I haven't started any organization. What do you want me to do with the money?" I asked.

"Well, I've been having this feeling like I should do something to contribute."

I was completely confused; and inside, my heart was telling me that this was the hand of God again. At this point, I was seriously overwhelmed with the things that God was doing in our lives. I honestly felt that God was rewarding me for my sacrifices. I also felt that God was giving me a wonderful ending to this part of my story because He knows and understands that this book has the ability to bring others to know Him.

We sent the cousin our account number so that he could wire money to us, and it was exactly the same amount of the salary that my husband used to get in the company.

After eight long months of waiting on the National Visa Center, on April 2, 2013, I called them and was told that our case was closed with them. That meant Albert's interview would be scheduled in the month of May and we would receive an email notifying us of the date. I called Albert right away to tell him. Each step that brought us closer to finishing the process gave me so much joy. One can't imagine that feeling unless they have walked through a situation like ours. I began to listen to one of my favorite songs by Juanita Bynum called "God of Second Chance!" While all alone in my room, I lifted my hands and allowed the tears to flow. I wanted to appreciate and worship God for how far He had brought us. All we had to do was put faith in Him and, of course, just live by his simple laws that only help us as humans.

God brought people into our lives to play the role that He wanted. Our close friends, whom we had met in Nigeria but had now moved to the U.S., told us that we should move to Missouri so we could be close to them. At one point, I did wonder where we would ever live when we moved back to America. We knew we didn't want to go back to Arkansas because of the old life we lived there. We also didn't have anybody else offering to help so we were glad for our dear friends in Christ who were arranging for the house that we would live in. All we had to do was send the money to pay for the rent; and, of course, God also provided the money for that. Every single area of this journey has been provided for through God, and I mean every single one. What greater joy can there be in knowing that there really is a God who cares for us and makes things possible when they seem impossible? "And we know that in all things God works for the good of those who love him, who have been called according to his purpose." Romans 8:28.

Finally, after eight years since my husband was deported, we received the date for his interview at the American Consulate in Lagos, Nigeria. This happened just after I had a dream that his interview date would be in March 2012; and in my dream I thought how that wasn't possible because it was so soon. But lo and behold, that was the date we actually received for his interview at the American Consulate in Lagos. Once again all funds were provided for us to make it happen: the trip to Lagos and back (11 hours away), the medical exam required, as well as housing and food.

Finally, we were able to submit the waiver that would prove the extreme hardship as it was our last step. Once again we had to wait to hear whether the waiver would be approved or denied. Initially, the form was supposed to take a maximum of five months, but since there had been a change in the immigration law and more people began applying for the same waiver, the form was going to take up to seven months. That news was a bit stressful for me since I had found out I was pregnant. I wanted the form to be approved in time for me to get to America to deliver my baby, and to be able to have my husband with me in the U.S. for the delivery.

After the experience I had delivering my son Micah in Nigeria, I did not want to deliver in Nigeria again. Our baby was due in December and if we were going to the U.S. based on the amount of time it would take for the form to be approved, then I would not make it in time. If I went to the States by myself, I would not have anywhere to stay while I waited to deliver. Then out of nowhere, our good friends that were kind enough to cosign for my husband, offered to let me to stay with them if necessary.

We began planning for my flight back to the U.S. I would stay with our friends and deliver our baby. Although I was grateful to have a place to stay, I was a bit heartbroken because it would mean that Albert would not be with me during the delivery and experience the joy of the birth. I would also be leaving my children behind. A part of me felt bad to even go to America and enjoy anything without my children. The mere thought of being away from them hurt me deeply since we didn't know how long we would have to be apart. During the time apart, Albert would have to work and take care of the house and the kids by himself. I would not be able to fulfill my role as a mother and a wife, and the thought hurt me once again.

I decided to try one more time to see if I get the case expedited. I contacted the Senator in Missouri where we planned to move. I wrote a letter detailing the violence, bombings, the lack of quality education for my children, and so on. I asked if the decision of the waiver could be expedited according to the circumstances. The Senator contacted the USCIS with my request, and again I had to wait to hear back from them. The waiting part became so difficult.

Eventually the USCIS office contacted me saying that the Senator's office should hear back from them in a week. So I waited a week and heard nothing. I was becoming impatient, weak, and tired.

A day came when I felt that I couldn't handle the waiting and having our lives in limbo. I cried hard on September 19. I cried out to God and told Him how tired I was and I needed Him to intervene. I told Him that the ending of my story is not supposed to be that I will leave my family and we will be separated for several months. I didn't stay in Nigeria for eight years to keep us together so at the end we would be split up. Shortly after I cried out to God, I checked the USCIS website and saw that our waiver was approved. I almost couldn't believe it. I jumped up to check the case number to make sure I had it correct. It was the most weird and amazing feeling in this world. I had waited for this day for almost a decade. I did not even sleep that night after hearing that finally it had been approved. I had worked hard and my writing skills helped us. Expedites are rarely granted, but when they read my expedite request it was approved in three weeks. The form itself was approved in just three months when others currently are waiting up to seven months. Finally, I felt like I could rest.

Then we realized that we had to wait for the American Consulate to actually contact my husband to request that he send them his passport, and we were not sure how long that would take. At the same time, since I was seven months pregnant, we knew that I would have to leave soon because the airline would not allow me to travel after eight months in the pregnancy. That seemed like another stress since our flight would be up to 30 hours with layovers and I was big and pregnant traveling around the world.

Not knowing how long would it would take for the Consulate to contact him, we didn't know whether I should make plans and take the children with me. The thought of my husband not being able to come along was stressful. I just felt like it would be a wonderful ending to my story if we could all go back together....like a fairy tale! I love my husband so much that I hate it when he is not by my side! I will do anything for my family, and neither my heart nor my soul is at peace when we are apart. This is the family with which God has blessed me!

Once again, God was just in time. Albert called to tell me that the Consulate called him to collect his passport! Praise God! He has been so good to me and my family. We found out that we would be able to travel together. It was like a fairy tale after all, with a happy ending! Romans 8:28 says, "And we know that in all things God works for the good of those who love him and have been called according to his purpose."

Now that the Consulate had contacted Albert, we could start selling the things in our house as well as our car, and looking for a renter for our house. This would help finance our move back to America, including buying our airline tickets. I sat right down with my laptop and started posting things for sale on an email group for the missionaries in Jos. Within one week I had sold everything in the house. While I dealt with the things in the house, Albert was running errands and trying to get the car sold and the house rented. We needed to purchase our tickets as soon as possible in order to get the best price. Eventually someone said they wanted to rent the house and someone else wanted to buy the car.

Our date was set to fly out of Jos to Lagos on October 14, 2013. We had to make sure everything was settled by that date. We were able to get our tickets to Lagos, but still needed to purchase four tickets to America from Nigeria. Just as we thought all was going smoothly, the people who had said they would buy the car and rent the house canceled at the last minute. We were worried, but God is always on time. Albert's cousin phoned to say he wanted to pay for the kids' tickets. Finally we were able to purchase our tickets. Imagine, after all those years of wondering how it would ever be possible, God made it happen.

At the same time, our great friends in Springfield, MO, (the ones we initially met in Nigeria) were helping us find a house to live in when we arrived. I didn't care if we didn't have any furniture in the house as long as we had a place to call home once again. The money we made from selling our things in Nigeria gave us enough to buy beds, a dining room table, a fridge, and coffee table. And Albert surprised me with a washer and dryer since I had longed to be able to use one again. Then we would be able to pay the rent and deposit once we arrived. Amazingly, the landlord was willing to hold the house for us and wait to be paid until we would arrive a month later. That was another one of God's blessings in our lives. Our friends helped us by moving everything into the house before we arrived.

The Consulate didn't have Albert's visa available in time for us to travel; so we had to reschedule Albert's ticket to arrive a few days after us. I did not enjoy the thought of traveling alone with the kids while I was 33 weeks pregnant, but I didn't care because we were near the end of the long journey and he would join us a few days later.

Finally it was time for the children and me to catch our flight after being in Lagos for a week. The airline needed a statement from my doctor saying that I was fit to fly in my pregnancy. I handed the letter to them and the supervisor asked how far along I was. I told her that I was at 33 weeks. She said I would have to go see their doctor who would determine if that was correct and to ascertain that I was indeed fit to fly since I was over 32 weeks. Apparently, after 32 weeks, a letter must be sent from the doctor directly to the main office of Dakar Airlines, and that the letter had to be less than 10 days old, something of which we were totally unaware. So we went to the room where we had been directed, and found a huge number of people trying to get in. Nobody was in a line; instead everybody was fighting to make it to the doorway of the room. There was no way I could have worked my way through the crowd, but Albert was there to fight his way through.

I made it inside the room and it seemed to be the hottest place I had ever entered. The nurse told me to lie down on the bed, and then she pressed on the top and bottom of my stomach and immediately she said that I was 38 weeks pregnant. I was so astonished that my mouth dropped open. If she pronounced that assumption, the airline wouldn't allow me to travel at all. I saw the doctor and asked him to come over so that I could explain what was going on. He asked me the date of my last menstrual period, did some calculations to figure my due date, and then stated that I was 34 weeks along. I insisted that I was not 34, but 33, weeks pregnant. Finally he told me to go and tell them I was 34 weeks. I looked at him in confusion and told him I needed a note or something or how would they know that I had even seen him. So he followed me to tell the supervisor and he refused to allow me to fly. Albert spent an hour begging him to allow me to fly, but he refused.

Consequently, we missed our flight and had to go find a doctor in Lagos to give us yet another letter stating that I was fit to fly. We had to pay to change our tickets, and that was money we needed for the move into our new home. We were completely exhausted and tired and ready to be settled. I needed a cold drink and an air conditioner.

God provided for our needs and we got word that our car had sold. We were able to purchase the tickets, the doctor's letter cleared me, and we all flew back to America together. I was completely exhausted after the extremely long flight and my feet were so swollen I could barely walk; but finally getting to America was completely worth it.

We arrived at our new home in Missouri. It was unbelievable to see that the house was completely set up and livable. We had everything we needed to live comfortably. There was even food in the fridge. Every food that I had missed for the past eight years was inside the fridge or in the pantry. And my favorite food, tacos and cheese dip, was already cooked and waiting for us. The beds were made with clean sheets and blankets; somebody gave us two desks, a couch and a love seat; and small things that were needed such as laundry detergent, soap for bathing, towels, pots, pans, glasses, plates, bowls, broom, coffee pot, crockpot, and so much more. The transition was so smooth, thanks to people we knew and even many we didn't know.

I took my first hot shower. I woke up the middle of the night and ate Doritos and drank a Dr Pepper. It was blissful.

Soon it was time to get the kids in school and get situated into the American culture. The only thing we needed desperately was a car. We were still waiting for our house in Nigeria to rent so we could buy a car. We were beginning to worry. Our friends let us use their kids' car for a few weeks, but they needed it back. As usual, just in time, our house in Nigeria was rented and we were able to buy a minivan. Even the vehicle we bought had to have been God-sent because of the reasonable price and because it was in great shape. Finally, it felt like things were complete.

To my surprise, I started missing Nigeria after a very short time. I now had two homes, Nigeria and America. It felt great to return to America with a renewed mind and as a better person with a completely different outlook than before. I was now torn between the things that I loved about both countries.

A week after our arrival, many of my extended family members from my mother's side of the family came to visit and welcome us. It was such a blessing and an honor.

Our son was born on December 10, 2013, and we named him Jayden Oluwatosin Owonubi. Jayden means "Jehovah had heard!" and Oluwatosin means "God is worthy of worship!" Ironically, He was dedicated to the Lord by Reverend Scott Ennis, the same person who dedicated Micah in Nigeria.

19

God brought me out of my old life into something greater than I ever could have imagined. Today I give Him all the glory and the honor for what He has done in my life. If not for Him, there is no telling where my life would have ended up. People from America wondered how I could live in such tough conditions in Nigeria. They made it known that they could never do it. However, a person can never predict how they will cope in any given circumstances until they are faced with them.

On the other hand, the Nigerians respected me and highly commended me for coming to live in their country when I could have avoided it. I could have easily chosen to go back to America, with or without our children; but I knew my decisions would shape my children's lives. It took me many years to realize that Nigeria was the best thing that ever happened to me. Believe it or not, even though I went through many struggles while adjusting to a new culture, I had a better life in Nigeria than I did in America. Albert had been right. There is more to life than material things such as running water, electricity and a fridge full of food. If you don't have Jesus in your life, it is meaningless.

People were surprised to see that I lived like a Nigerian for so many years, but they didn't know my background. Yes, I came from America, the land of milk and honey. However, I came from a painful past, a less-than-ideal childhood. I spent many years holding onto the wounds of my childhood. I needed to be removed far enough away from my old life to be able to see clearly—and I needed Jesus in my life to make that change. I wanted something different for my children. I wanted to succeed in life and overcome my past. I did not want to run away from my problems anymore.

There were many times while living in Nigeria that I just wanted to give up and go back to my country, my comfort zone. But then I would consider what the effects would be on my marriage and on my children. I have come to realize something very important: *It's not about us; it's about them!* It is easy to become selfish, thinking about our own feelings, and neglecting to realize the consequences it will have on our children. I spent many years dwelling on how the people in my life had hurt me. I spent years focusing on what people were not doing for me. I lived in bondage by holding onto the past. Not letting go hindered my growth. I decided to make conscious, positive choices so there would be no negative effects on my children. One day we will die and leave behind our children, the ones Albert and I brought into this world with the help of God.

I give God the honor and the glory for our lives, our marriage, and our wonderful children. I couldn't have survived a day of living in Nigeria without Jesus in my life. He was obviously watching over me since the day I was born, trying to rescue me from the dangers and pain of this world, and waiting for me to say the "I do," that I would give my life to Him and let Him guide my steps. Because of Him, my marriage will last. Because of Him, my children will not grow up in a broken home. Because of Him, my children will obtain a college degree (while being encouraged by their parents). And because of Him, my children will grow up in a stable home and learn to have their own relationships with Him. Today I cry tears of joy for the story that my Lord Jesus Christ has given me to tell the world. Mission accomplished! Through Christ, I managed to break the chains which had bound my family for generations. I am the first in my family to get an education, and the first in my family to refuse divorce in spite of overwhelming obstacles. I managed to break the chains of racism. I know the effects that divorce, abuse, and rejection have on children; but those events do not have to prevent me from doing what is right and fulfilling God's purpose for my life. I don't even want to think about how my life would have been different if I had decided not to follow my husband to Nigeria, and if we hadn't given our lives to Christ when we did.

I am grateful to my Lord for my marriage and how He has stitched our wounds and they have healed. I thank God for giving me a wonderful husband that understands me and strives to be the best father and husband that he can be. I honestly couldn't ask for a better husband. This journey to Nigeria has proven our love for each other. We allowed our struggles to bring us closer to each other instead of splitting us apart; we couldn't have done it without Him, Jesus Christ!

My husband once looked at me and said, "You are so beautiful!"
As I smiled back, I said, "Thank You!"
He continued to look at me saying, "I have always been attracted to you, but the person that you have become has helped me to see how beautiful you really are!"

I am so grateful for the opportunity to have spent all those years in Nigeria. I am proud to be married into the Nigerian culture. I am now amazed that I once actually thought it was a disaster to have to live in a country where all my comforts were taken away from me. I even wondered how I got suckered into such suffering, but that was just the devil trying to steer me away from the real truth. God had a plan for my life and the devil knew what my God was trying to do. God renewed my mind, opened my eyes, and changed my life. He gave me a husband that loves me and understands me and also shares the same focus in life. Thanks to the power of Christ in our lives, we are both committed to our marriage and want to spend the rest of our lives serving God. We do not want to be lost again.

God replaced my tears of pain and rejection with joy by bringing me to a wonderful country with great people. Even as I am writing today, it still hurts that my father has never met my husband. It hurts that my husband's parents and my mother are no longer alive to be grandparents to our children. It hurts that none of my family from America ever called to ask how we were doing. I do know that God loves me and I trust that he knows what is best for my life. The pain of this world will never stop; it is a part of life. But I can use that pain to grow and learn from my experiences. The events in my life made me who I am today.

I began to thank God for the opportunity for my children to grow up in Nigeria in the early childhood years, to live in a country where they are not rejected for the color of their skin. Instead they are appreciated for their light skin. My children have an identity. They know that they are American, but their black roots can be traced from the Yoruba tribe where they come from, a village called Ogidi, a village where they will be accepted for who they are.

Our closest loved ones may hurt us. Some people will not be happy for our success in life. My family members didn't seem to be happy for me. They seemed to enjoy seeing me when I was a failure and when I was unhappy. The only person I ever knew that was truly happy for me was my husband. He knew where I came from and where I was going in life. God extended my family to include the many Nigerians who frequently asked me, "How are your studies?"

and "How is the book coming along?" The people who should mean the most to me didn't seem to be happy for me. It hurts, but I cannot allow those people to control my thoughts and actions.

It is Satan's plan to destroy us after all that we have been through and overcome. We rebuke him in Jesus' name! We will continue on with the life that God gave us without letting the devil win victory over our lives. We are letting God win the battle. Even though we were hurt deeply and often felt like giving up, Jesus has never failed us. He forgives us. He is patient, loving, and kind. He wants us to have abundant life. I refuse to allow anything or anyone to get in the way of fulfilling my purpose in this life. I want people to speak good things about me when I die. I want to leave an impact on the lives of people I touch.

I trust God that one day my father will agree to meet my husband. And if that is not the will of God, I trust that He will heal my wounds. I respect my father's wishes although it hurts deeply. I understand what it was like not to know who Jesus Christ is. I know that my father is human, I understand that he cannot help how he was taught; after all he grew up in a time where racism was freely practiced. How can I not forgive him? After all, God forgave me for all of my sins!

We gave our lives to Christ, so now our children will grow up learning about Jesus; how he died on the cross for our sins, rose from the dead, and left behind His wonderful book called the Bible to guide us through our lives. He also gave me the courage to write this book to tell my story. It is my hope that I will help someone who has gone through similar circumstances to see that we do not have to allow the events of our past to overpower us.

Every day that I wake up and go to sleep, I no longer allow the devil to overcome my mind, making me think that I am nobody, or that I am useless and will not accomplish anything in my life. I no longer allow him to corrupt my mind. Instead I allow Jesus Christ to fill me with His Spirit; the Spirit that gives me hope and helps me not to be fearful, ungrateful, guilty, or selfish. He helps me release malice against those who have done wrong toward me. I pray for their souls and I pray they will also forgive me for my wrongs.

I eventually realized how much power I have over my emotions. I could have chosen to be miserable the entire time I was in Nigeria, but instead I chose to be happy and make the best of my situation. I chose to look at the opportunities set before me rather than my circumstances. It was all about changing my mindset and perspective. We choose the lens through which we view life. My past experiences have shaped me, but will never destroy me!

Just as God helped me, He can help you through any situation. There is nothing impossible for Him. Trust in the Lord always and lean not on your own understanding. Submit yourself to Him.

The world is a scary place without Jesus Christ. Without Him, we are without any direction for our lives; but He provides hope through our struggles, heartaches, and pain. The Bible says in Jeremiah 29:11, "For I know the plans I have for you, declares the Lord, plans to prosper you and not to harm you, plans to give you a hope and a future." We may think that God has forgotten about us, but He never has. Luke 12:7 says, "...the very hairs of your head are all numbered." He wants us to acknowledge Him and submit to Him fully.

We cannot change our past, nor can we change anyone else. We cannot change the way our parents were raised. We cannot change the way they raised us, or the mistakes they made in the process. Every parent makes mistakes and there is no perfect parent. But with the help of God we CAN choose to make a change and ensure that we do not pass on the negative traits carried down to our generation. We can choose to break the chains!

There is no handbook that tells us how to raise our children, but God left behind a wonderful book full of instructions as to how we can live our lives. That book is the Bible. I cannot imagine raising my children without teaching them about Jesus. I want my children to know how to overcome the obstacles in their own lives. The Bible says that the hearts of men are desperately wicked.

It is not by mistake that God brought me to Nigeria where many people have a strong relationship with Jesus, and sent me to an Assemblies of God church after I spent my earliest childhood years in an Assemblies of God church in America. It is not by mistake that He placed key people in my life, provided for my ticket in order to reunite with my husband, and provided for our entire stay in Nigeria. It is not by mistake that I was able to finish my education. It is not by mistake that I married Laolu Albert Owonubi. None of the story is by mistake: everything happens for a reason, and everything happens in God's timing.

I am so grateful for my family in Nigeria, which is also my church family. Every time I attended church at Evangel Chapel, I held back my tears of joy. It is a wonderful experience to worship with people who know how to worship our God more than anyone in the world.

I thank God and Nigeria for being my Good Samaritan. Sometimes I must allow a few of those tears of joy to seep out. I am overwhelmed with the love that comes from Christ. I am overwhelmed to think of what my life would have been like if He had not intervened, and if I hadn't finally chosen Him instead of running away from my problems.

I love to see how the Nigerians put all of their energy into dancing for Jesus. It is the same energy that is used to dance in a club, yet it is motivated by their love for God and it amazes me. It brings me great joy to be among the Nigerians, even when I am the only white person in the entire church. Nigeria will always have a place in my heart. Nigeria has left a permanent mark on my life by showing love in times of trouble and hardship.

It brought me great joy to see my daughter on Children's Day in church after she had memorized twenty-five lesson topics from the Sunday school manual and their accompanying verses. It brought me great joy to see my daughter singing, "I want to be thankful, I want to be grateful! I like to think about the goodness of the Lord, He gives me everything I need and so much more!" in a school program at the end of year. I tried to hold back the tears from running down my face. I didn't want the people around me to wonder what was wrong with me. I was just so happy and grateful that this was the outcome of my daughter's life. I knew that if she grew up in America, the story could be different since public schools no longer teach about the Bible or allow prayer in the classroom.

It brought me great joy when Micah was just three years old and he made a cross with two sticks, laid them on the ground and said, "Jesus died on the cross!" My heart swelled with joy when he would shout, "Praise, Praise, Praise the Lord!" Both of my children often go around singing to the Lord. Whitney often wakes us up to tell us it's time to pray. Instead of playing games with her friends, she gives a devotion teaching them about the Word of God. She writes poems and songs about Jesus and sings them in her room.

If I was brought to Nigeria for no other reason, it means my children will grow up in the fear of the Lord. They will learn about what Jesus did for us and what He wants for our lives. This is the best gift I could ever give Whitney and Micah. When the time is right, they will each receive a copy of this book to see how God changed my life in spite of my background.

The journey is not over yet. I am just beginning my journey. The journey God has planned for you is also just beginning. He is reaching out His hand, ready to carry you along your own journey whenever you are ready to follow. Why not take His hand and see what the Lord has in store for you.

The End

Acknowledgements

This has got to be the most arduous project I have ever undertaken; and after two years this book is finally being published. I wish to take a moment to pay homage to those who truly believed in this project. It is never an easy thing to share your life with the entire world, but I do believe that our stories are meant to be shared so that others who have gone through similar situations can relate, find hope, and be inspired.

First and foremost, I must give all honor and glory to God. He has taken me to great places and changed my life. He forgave me for all my wrongs and shed light into my life to help me to see what needed to be done. He has led me to a perfect peace.

To my husband Albert, I thank God for putting you in my life. You have been so good to me even though the beginning of our relationship was rocky when we were so young. Our lives and our marriage changed drastically when he called us to go to Nigeria. Albert, I thank you for never giving up on me. You believed in me and you encouraged me to get my education and to write this book. Thank you for your patience with me on the days I ignored you and the kids while I was doing my schoolwork or writing this story. Thank you for seeing the best in me regardless of my background or where I came from. And thank you for giving this book its wonderful title that fits the story just perfectly.

To Mary Beth Oyebade, you and your mother were the first ones to lay eyes on my manuscript. I know it was a complete mess in the beginning, but you didn't give up on me. Thank you for encouraging me that day you set aside to meet with me to discuss what I needed to do to further my goal in publishing. You will always have a special place in my heart for being there for me when I was going through the culture shock of being in Nigeria. You helped make my days brighter and became a great influence in my life. It was surely part of God's plan for us to cross paths.

To Sandi Wallestad, (Mary Beth's mom) you have been so passionate about helping me edit my book. I don't know what I have would have done without you. You must have gone through it more than anybody. You were always willing to help me in any way you could. You completed the job of editing and left it as a great work of art. You also encouraged me to continue on with publishing when I was discouraged. You told me that this is a story that needs to be shared and for me to tell the devil to move on.

To LaVonna Ennis, you were the very first one to edit the manuscript. You met it at its worst and I am certain it was not an easy process for you. You took the time to help regardless of your busy schedule as a pastor's wife, student, and mother. You and your family will also always have a special place in my heart. You met us when we were babies in Christ and watched us grow. Not only did you watch us, but you helped us. You helped us in so many ways that I get a tingling in my heart when I look at a picture of you and your family. When I wondered if anybody in America cared, you changed that and let me know that somebody does care.

To Rick Jara, thank you for taking the picture of me with Micah on my back in the village of Ganawuri. Neither of us ever knew that it would be the front cover of my book one day. And thank you for helping with ideas for the book cover and actually doing the final work for both the interior and exterior. I am so grateful.

To Richard Snyder for allowing me to use his pictures from his photography page on Facebook:
https://www.facebook.com/RSnyder.Photography

I must also always remember each and every person that God appointed to play a part in helping our family: Folake and Femi Ehindero, Marybeth and the Niger Wives that had a quick going away get-together for me and gave us a gift card to Walmart (wink wink), Grace Olukoya and her husband, The Ennis family, Sarah and Uche Ejiro, Gina and Emmanuel Samci, Olufemi Ladeji, Ceceilia and Modupe Ladeji, Mommy Dupe, Justin and Amber Hoppe, Debbie Kay Colbert, Chai Gang, as well as the extended Owonubi family, and if there is anybody that I may have forgotten, I am thankful for you as well.

And of course, thank you to all who took the time to read my manuscript and/or write your owns words of what you saw in the story: my husband Albert, Reverend Godswill Israel, Sarah Ajero, LaVonna Ennis, Mary Beth Oyebade, Sandi Wallestad, and Ayo Owonubi, you all encouraged me greatly.

30784464R00089

Made in the USA
Charleston, SC
25 June 2014